IN THE
MEANTIME

IN THE
MEANTIME

40 BIBLICAL
MEDITATIONS
ON ORDINARY,
EVERYDAY LIFE

Keith J White

WTL PUBLICATIONS

TO MY FIVE DEAR GRANDCHILDREN
ISAAC, MEGAN, FLORENCE, OLIVE AND NATHAN
WITH WHOM THE EVERYDAY IS SO OFTEN
FULL OF WONDER

In the Meantime
Forty biblical meditations on ordinary, everyday life

Published by WTL Publications Ltd
10 Crescent Road, South Woodford, London E18 2JB

ISBN 978 095647572 5
First published 2013
10 9 8 7 6 5 4 3 2 1 0

A catalogue record for this book is available from the British Library

Cover picture: Looking west from Moelwyn Bach
All photos were taken in North Wales by Keith J. White or Tony Cantale
Book design by Tony Cantale

For further copies or information
call +44 20 8504 2702,
email enquiries@wtlpublications.co.uk
or visit www.wtlpublications.co.uk

Printed in UK by Lightning Source

www.wtlpublications.co.uk

CONTENTS

Introduction

HOW ORDINARY IS ORDINARY?

This book has a simple message: once we begin to explore the meaning of mundane, everyday life, to value it and try to understand what God might be doing and saying through it, and how we are to live each day with integrity and hope, then a whole new world begins to open up. Most of life for a Christian (as for anyone else) is ordinary, in the sense that it is made up largely of routine and unexceptional actions and thought. If, instead of longing for miracles, revivals and dramatic revelations, we pause to reflect on everyday life, we open ourselves to the realisation that there is, despite all the evidence to the contrary, no part or period of human existence where God is not present. The Kingdom of Heaven is characterised by small things, little people, and ordinary happenings, and has very different time-spans and processes to what we expect. To glimpse it therefore requires the eyes and ears of faith in the midst of messy and unexceptional life.

Of course we treasure the special times and we celebrate the extraordinary events, but it is not healthy to assume that they are, or to long that they should be, the staple spiritual and emotional diet of our lives. In this process of letting go, we allow what is heavenly and divine to shine through, and out of, the routine of daily life. The whole world, whether skies, shook foil or clods of earth, becomes "charged with the grandeur of God", not just the mountain top experiences of the Trans-figuration of Jesus, or God speaking at Sinai.

Many others have pondered the ordinary, in-between times: the limbo and the liminal. Thomas Kuhn rewrote the history of science by examining the periods when an old paradigm was in crisis, and before a new paradigm became established. Victor Turner studied rites of passage and what happened between one life-stage and the inauguration of the next. Both found that historians tend to pay attention to the discoveries and discoverers (in the case of science), or the coming of age (in the case of life rituals), rather than what actually went on in the untidy and unfinished period before the new era was established. The overarching meta-narrative of "progress" is so pervasive in the twenty-first century, that we find it hard to incorporate experiences of stagnation, frustration, indeterminacy and regress, into it. Yet these are the stuff of real life both for individuals, and also for social groups.

THE GERM OF THE IDEA

On reflection I think it was probably on a flight back from Moscow in the twilight of the Communist era that the first seed of this book was sown. I had been visiting Russian Christians together with a personal friend of mine. We were worn out by a week of late night conversations, and apprehensive about the changes obviously coming to this vast nation. Mikhail Gorbachev was still president of the Soviet Union, but his days were obviously numbered. As we headed over the Baltic Sea and into the darkening night sky we chatted perhaps more openly than ever before. After a long sleep under the opium of Communism, Russia was stirring into life. Founded on a lie, virtually the whole of the twentieth century had been a dark age. What the future held, who knew? A mighty edifice was crumbling and a new era was beginning to emerge from under the rubble.

It was an exciting, historic, momentous time to be in Moscow. There was something of the atmosphere of Pentecost in the air with all the heightened emotions, convictions, tensions and creativity of the early chapters of Acts. The winter of communist rule was nearly over. Springtime would be painful as the thaw set in, but it was coming. As the British Airways jet crossed the North Sea our thoughts and conversation began to turn towards life in England. When compared with the vast, almost tectonic, changes erupting in Russia our lives whether in church, families or communities would be comparatively calm, quiet and uneventful. We were heading back to ordinary life in the peaceful country that Edmund Burke portrayed unforgettably as not given to revolutions or major upheavals.

Despite our interest in and commitment to Christians in Russia, we both felt our vocation was to live and serve in the comparatively uneventful life of England. And as I pondered this contrast I realised that it is the calling of most Christians most of the time, whether we live in periods of great upheaval or stability, to be faithful and responsible in the ordinary, mundane affairs of daily existence. Between the memorable personal events and life stages from birth to death, there are years of childhood which seem at the time to be endless, then, for some, parenthood, for some work or unemployment, weekly patterns of sleeping and rising, caring and shopping, work and holidays, repairs and tidying, planting and weeding. Most lives never make a headline even in the local paper, and history bears virtually no trace of their existence apart from official records of births, marriages and deaths. They are epitomised by Dorothea in George Eliot's novel *Middlemarch*.

And what is true of individuals is also true of communities, churches and nations. Like the Soviet Union, they have their great turning points or events that are remembered because recorded, and yet most of the time they are occupied with routines: the seasons of the year, balancing the books, the maintenance of systems, managing minor change, coping with leaders, communities, governments which are neither visionary nor dictatorial, but competent in some respects and leaving something to be desired in others.

Most of life is lived in what I came to recognise and term the "meantime", when although there is an awareness of, even respect for events of the past, and consciousness that there may well be significant changes ahead, the stuff of life is to be found in "between-times": getting on quietly with the demands and adapting to the patterns of ordinary existence. And that became clear to me because the Russia we were leaving behind was at a momentous point of its history, while the England we were heading for was at a more settled period in its life and development. Should we therefore assume that God's presence and his Kingdom are more in evidence in one than the other?

It was this dramatic contrast that also helped me to see that the way we often tend to handle the Bible, whether in corporate worship or personal devotions, is by turning to and feeding upon that which is extraordinary rather than that which is normal. A recent sermon was a case in point: it was based on the call of Gideon, and the famous rout of the Midianites by just three hundred men (Judges 6 and 7). It was used as the basis for us trusting God to supply us with what was needed to carry out the tasks he calls us to. This dramatic incident was preceded by seven years of oppression and followed by forty years of peace, but neither were referred to.

In addition to the story of Gideon momentous events in the thousands of years that the Bible covers include: Creation, the Flood, the call of Abraham, the exodus of the people of Israel from Egypt, the conquest of the Promised Land, the reigns of David and Solomon, the destruction of Jerusalem, the Exile, the rebuilding of the city, the life of Christ, Pentecost and the growth of the church, and the journey of Paul to Rome. The supernatural and extraordinary events tend to cluster at a few points of the story: Moses and Joshua, Elijah and Elisha, Jesus and the apostles. For the rest history seems to take its course, full of ups and downs, twists and turns, and periods when little of note or special significance seems to be happening.

Let's look at a few examples using the biblical timescale. (It is immaterial for this purpose whether we read it literally or metaphorically: the message is the same.) Adam is known primarily for disobeying God in a moment of time. We often tend to overlook the 930 years he lived. (It was 130 years before Seth was born!) Noah was 500 years old before the flood came. There are hundreds of unrecorded years between the Flood and the call of Abraham. Abraham was 75 when he set out from Haran. He lived for another 100 years. Isaac was 60 before we hear anything of his life. The Israelites lived in Egypt for 430 years and little of this history is recorded before the story of the exodus begins. Moses lived for 40 years in Egypt before he fled to Midian. He was a shepherd in Midian for 40 years. So he was 80 before he began the task for which he is remembered. He died at the age of 120 years. The 40 years the Israelites spent in the wilderness are one of the best-known periods of "ordinariness" – but we tend to envisage them as quite extraordinary given Sinai, the Tabernacle and the miracles including those of the supply of water from the rock, manna, and quails. Joshua died aged 110 and for much of his life he was inactive. We don't know how long.

One scheme of dates (*NIV Study Bible,* p.322) suggests that 480 years elapsed between the exodus and the fourth year of Solomon's reign. The events described in the interim leave huge tracts of this period unrecorded. King Ahab died in 853 B.C. and the fall of Jerusalem was in 586 B.C. Throughout this period the whole reign of a king is often summed up in a few words and no special events are recorded. According to Jeremiah the exile lasts for seventy years and is followed by 150 years with bursts of activity, including that led by Ezra and Nehemiah. The four hundred years from the time of Nehemiah until the birth of Jesus (the inter-testamental period) are sometimes called the "Silent Years" because they are not recorded in our Bible.

In the life of Jesus thirty years are covered with barely a mention, and in the life of Paul there are periods of silence including the best part of fourteen years (Galatians 2:1). Though some would argue about particular dates and periods, these are the figures actually recorded at some point of the Bible and so they are significant whether taken literally or symbolically. Thus the pattern is clear: there are substantial periods of time in individual lives, and the history of God's people, devoid of special events or prophesies and when little or nothing is recorded.

By way of contrast the dramatic and speedy rescue of the Hebrews from captivity in Egypt is mentioned hundreds of times throughout the Bible. It is still celebrated weekly and annually by the Jewish community. And it is understandable that we celebrate and rejoice in the special events like the exodus. They are occasions that reveal particular insights into God's heart and will. We draw comfort and inspiration from them. Yet they can be so attractive and memorable that there is the risk that we take them, even mistake them, for what is normal. Generations of Hebrews cried out to the Lord their God for liberation from slavery, and the two generations we remember in liturgy, sermons, and celebrations, are the parents and children of those who survived Passover Night and crossed the Red Sea.

We admire and venerate Moses, the leader of these liberated people. But most of us are not all called to be a Moses: his encounter with Yahweh beside the burning bush was an exceptional moment even for this exceptional man. His successor, Joshua, was one of the all-time greats of biblical history. And we can follow the chequered political story of this nation by naming Gideon, David, Solomon, Hezekiah and Josiah. They stand out from the mediocre leaders. All of these are accompanied and often chastened and challenged by those called the prophets. They include three towering giants: Jeremiah, Ezekiel, and Isaiah. It is right and proper to let these great figures speak to our inner beings, but in doing so we must be careful not to assume they represent the normal spiritual life. We are not all Isaiah, and his encounter with the living God in the temple (Isaiah 6) was exceptional even for him.

PONDERING CHRISTIAN LIFE IN THAT LIGHT

It may be that readers can agree broadly with this overview, without being greatly surprised. Even if it comes from a different angle to most perspectives on the Scriptures, why should it pose a problem? This is when a cursory glance at much Christian devotional literature, commentaries and biographies is salutary: one could be forgiven for thinking that we are expected to be exceptional people or groups, encountering great events or experiences year by year, if not week by week. Some churches consequently seem to depend on something new on the horizon all the time, and what is true for the community is assumed to be true also for the individual Christian. Post-Pentecost ordinary life as responsible and godly pupils, parents and citizens is not good enough. Unless there are tangible and continual signs of blessing then something is wrong.

Of course not all branches and traditions of the Christian faith assume this. The monastic orders are especially important here in that they stress pattern and order, simple living and ordinary tasks. There is also a contemplative tradition based on the acceptance of the here and now, the significance of being as distinct from doing or planning. But by their very nature they do not grab the headlines unlike the "Toronto Blessing", a "revival", "answers to prayer", miracles, or a pilgrimage. Thus many Christians receive, whether consciously or unconsciously, an unbalanced diet of teaching, reading or preaching consisting mostly of special signs of life and growth.

The implication, whether or not it is actually stated, is that the extraordinary should be the daily experience of the church. The effect on both individuals and churches is not hard to deduce. There is a sense of guilt and uncertainty: "What do you want us to do now, Lord?" "Is it me that is holding back the promised blessing?" "Why is there such blessing in other places, but not my life and church?" Thus a weight of expectation is placed on believers: a tension between the realities of their daily lives, and the models that are extolled week by week. This tension is the stuff of something like neurosis: its hallmark is that it tends to undervalue if not undermine daily life and experience. The roles, responsibilities and tasks of everyday life - parent, child, work colleague, neighbour, are over-shadowed by the exceptional encounters of the great biblical characters. (It should be remarked in passing that all this is not helped by the cult of celebrity that characterises so much of the life portrayed by the contemporary media.) Meanwhile the constant reminders of God's presence - the stars, children, the lilies, the seasons, his patterns, a meal, raindrops, shafts of sunlight, are all but irrelevant in the hankering after the super-natural.

FROM A NEW BIBLE TO FORTY MEDITATIONS

This series of meditations and reflections was written during a lengthy period of study (it lasted over twenty years) during which I was preparing a new edition of the Bible. The discipline of having to study every book, every chapter and every verse, forced me to reflect on the relation of the ordinary to the exceptional. And the result is a collection of meditations which friends and colleagues have told me speak to their daily lives as individuals and churches. Much of the Old Testament teaching applies to everyday life, especially Psalms, Proverbs and the Prophets, and much of the teaching of the New Testament likewise addresses ordinary personal and social life. It is for us to live in a new way, in a new light, but not expecting vast upheavals, changes, discoveries and revolutions just around every corner. They may come but we should not be thrown by them or depend on them. Our calling is to be faithful where God has placed us.

We live, as has so often been said, between the "Now" and "Not Yet" of God's kingdom. When Jesus entered history and the Spirit came at Pentecost the new kingdom was inaugurated. Eternal life is now. And yet the kingdom is not fully realised on earth. It is still to come. Our job is to occupy the space God has created for us between these two great cosmic events in and through Jesus. "Thine is the kingdom"…"Thy kingdom come". Some may find it helpful to think of the slack between the ebbing and flowing tides; or the stillness between waves of the sea. An image that V.S. Naipaul uses in his novel *The Mimic Men* is that of periods of life that are "in parenthesis". They are to all intents and purposes bracketed from any meaningful, purposeful activity that might be heading somewhere, or part of what might be recorded in a biography, let alone an autobiography.

Perhaps it is the very concept of the Kingdom of Heaven which creates a problem for us. We find it virtually impossible to separate God's humble, hidden, sacrificial way of doing things (as revealed uniquely and authoritatively in Jesus), from the power, hierarchies, splendour of human empires and nation-states. It does not take long to realise that by focusing on people like Moses, Joshua, David and Solomon, and events like the exodus and the occupation of the Promised Land can easily confuse the Kingdom of Heaven with earthly political or religious structures and events. For this reason some time ago I have found it helpful to refer to the Kingdom of Heaven as "where God has his way".

So, if we trust our Heavenly Father and believe that he is working his way in and through all things, we will know that he is active when we are not aware of it just as much, if not more than, in those moments or times of spiritual awareness. And this has critical implications for how we live when our lives seem to be stalled or in parenthesis. We are not as it were to sit back believing that he will work all things together without our contributions, or undervalue our lives during the slack, in between times. We will not be waiting for something to turn up that will give meaning to our lives. Rather we will seek to live lives that reflect and are consonant with the way he does things. We will accept his timing, and try to do everything to the best of our abilities.

George Herbert and Horatius Bonar got it just right in their hymns. In some ways this series of meditations is an extended reflection on the theme of these simple poems.

> Teach me, my God and King,
> in all things thee to see,
> and what I do in anything
> to do it as for thee.
>
> A man that looks on glass,
> on it may stay his eye;
> or if he pleaseth, through it pass,
> and then the heaven espy.
>
> All may of thee partake;
> nothing can be so mean,
> which with this tincture, "for thy sake,"
> will not grow bright and clean.
>
> A servant with this clause
> makes drudgery divine:
> who sweeps a room, as for thy laws,
> makes that and the action fine.
>
> This is the famous stone
> that turneth all to gold;
> for that which God doth touch and own
> cannot for less be told.
>   GEORGE HERBERT

Fill thou my life, O Lord my God
In every part with praise,
That my whole being may proclaim
Thy being and Thy ways.

Not for the lip of praise alone,
Nor e'en the praising heart:
I ask, but for a life made up
Of praise in every part.

Praise in the common things of life,
Its goings out and in;
Praise in each duty and each deed,
However small and mean.

Fill every part of me with praise:
Let all my being speak
Of Thee and of Thy love, O Lord,
Poor though I be and weak.

So shall Thou, gracious Lord, from me
Receive the glory due,
And so shall I begin on earth
The song forever new.

So shall no part of day or night
From sacredness be free,
But all my life, in every step
Be fellowship with Thee.
HORATIUS BONAR

What follows is written with the belief that, set in context, our daily lives with all their struggles, messiness, untidiness, failures and routines are always at the intersection of the natural and the supernatural, time and eternity, where God can have his way; that with the eyes of faith we can see God in all things; that time past and time future are both perhaps contained in time present and that here and now is where God has chosen us to be, not there and then. The meantime may seem ordinary to us and to others but to our Lord and Master it is no nearer or farther from his heart and grace than those moments of dazzling splendour and revelation. For us the ordinary is the *ground* of attention as we highlight the *figure* and focus on the exceptional; in God's sight *figure* and *ground* are interchangeable and equally precious.

Not long after touching down from Moscow I was leading worship and preaching at a church in East London, right by the park where the 2012 London Olympics were held. The theme of the service was one of those ordinary times in the Bible when nothing much was happening (at least to the people concerned) and in the course of the sermon I asked those whose lives were like jig-saw puzzles with one or more pieces missing at present to stay behind afterwards. Imagine my surprise when nearly half the congregation stayed to chat and pray! They couldn't see how God's plan for them was working out; they didn't find obvious fulfilment in what they were doing. They were looking for something else (job, partner, experience of God). And that was in a church where the minister had his feet pretty firmly on the ground. He had not been setting before them great visions of untold blessing and revivals. They told me how ordinary their lives and Christian experience had been for years.

Until we paused together to reflect on what this meant most had tended to assume that the missing piece would turn up, rather like Godot. As we shared together it began to dawn on us that this was to undervalue life as it was – the messiness and incompleteness of daily life. This book is written for this East-end fellowship and all who recognise, sometimes with humour, the mysteries and paradoxes of life, the pressures and longings, but who are prepared to accept the present as the setting in which God's glory is manifested – who see the meantime as valuable in itself, not just as a period after a big event or before the next. In other words it is dedicated to most Christians and most churches most of the time!

FINDING THE RIGHT SHAPE

It came as a surprise to discover that the hardest part of writing this book was not finding the content: there is plenty of that in daily life and the Scriptures. It was deciding on an appropriate shape or form. After all I could hardly look for the highlights and trace dramatic events and conflicts in the periods of ordinariness! It began as a study or analysis of the in-between periods of life, using traditional life-stages as a framework. Maybe that task is still to be undertaken. It was Christine Smith, a book editor who eventually suggested the idea of meditations, who provided the catalyst for the present structure. But there remained the question of how to divide or organise that which is essentially undefined and uneventful. I realised how linear novels and dramas are by their very nature. And academic studies are a different genre depending on a static form. By definition they are systematic. What was needed here was something with form but which could allow a multitude of allusions and associations – something like poetry. If I were a poet, perhaps like Herbert and Bonar, I would have written my thoughts in verse!

If you turn back to the contents page you will see the simple structure I have adopted, but a little explanation of the shape and order of the contents may help. It should be seen as playful rather than studious. I needed something like this to help my writing, but perhaps the reader can lay aside the form I had in my mind. To explain why I have chosen this structure is not meant to determine how the reader will respond to the contents. Significantly the heart, or centre, of the book is *being*. The book has a still point around which everything turns. It is not moving away from anything or towards a climax.

The section on being is one of five, each comprising eight meditations. (I had realised that there were forty meditations and rejoiced, because perhaps the most pervasive biblical symbol for the in-between times is "forty years" or "forty days"!) We begin with the process of *looking back*, and end with *looking forward*. This is reassuring in that it resonates with our linear expectations, and places *being* – that is the present moment – in a familiar context. What then to do with *doing*? There was a temptation to leave it out completely because so much attention is given to it in other literature. Whether one thinks of management, health, education, parenting, sport or religion, so much assumes action and effort. On the other hand the everyday is made up of a myriad of little acts or actions, some conscious, others reflex or routine. (Wordsworth wrote of them as: "that best portion of a good man's life, his little, nameless, unremembered, acts of kindness and of love": *Lines Written above Tintern Abbey*). I have placed *doing* before *being* therefore not out of priority but because, in my view, we need to move through *doing* before we come to *being*.

And that left *going astray*, a series of reflections, possibly the most marginalised of them all. For even in the West there is a recognition that we must move from *doing* to *being* in order to realise our human potential, to empathise and sympathise, as individuals and friends. But why include failure and sin in such meditations? Because it is an essential element of our humanity, part of the painful process of gestation and growth, and comprises much of the content of the Scriptures. It is fruitless to ask how life might have been. We can only sharpen our insight into how it has been and how it is. The biblical record tells of a God who has chosen to create a world with freedom to think, to imagine, to create, and therefore to go astray, as one of its most precious but dangerous elements. And humans, like sheep, are prone to go off-track. Often our focus is on how on the one hand we prevent sinning, and on the other how we deal with the effects of sin (two parameters of the sinful act: temptation and atonement). Our focus in this section is rather more on how even sin can be understood and incorporated into a process (though painful and hurtful to self, others and God) of gestation and growth.

This is, of course, controversial and risky. But as I have reflected on the whole compass of Scripture and continued to study world history I cannot but marvel at the way it is often the periods of frustration, suffering and persecution that turn out with hindsight to contribute to understanding and growth. This is not the place to add another chapter to attempted theologies of suffering, but let us rest with these thoughts: the holocaust has been seen perhaps as one of the defining points of twentieth century western history. How can we explore everyday life with integrity if we neglect suffering epitomised so comprehensively by this period of European history? Where was God as the young Jewish man convulsed on the gallows? If we dare to believe that God was in Christ and through his suffering, wounds, stripes we are healed, then we must however falteringly believe that God was in the suffering, convulsing with the dying man. Whole nations may have gone astray for periods of their history, but that does not mean that God is a detached judge.

This then is why the meditations are ordered as they are. But you are invited to be as free to roam in reading them, as I was in writing them. Why not choose your own order? I would be delighted to hear how you plotted or discovered your own route through them: where you paused, what you omitted.

THE PRAYERS

Finally I offer a word about the prayers. Please ignore them completely if they seem irrelevant or inappropriate. I have often been on the brink of deleting them. Some friends advised me to, but others found them integral to the meditations. As I have re-visited and re-written them, over and over again, I have found them somehow helpful even if I fail to understand why. They represent an imaginary conversation with my Heavenly Father. Could I stress the *imaginary* nature? Given the frailty and limitations of human thought, it must be underlined that I am not attempting to speak for or on behalf of God in these prayers: more accurately, to encourage the reader to consider what the conversation might be like in his or her case.

The prayers probably owe much to the prayer life of my grandmother. After she became a widow she occupied a bedroom on the floor beneath mine. She was very deaf and her prayers seemed to be uttered with the unconscious assumption that God must be deaf too! Each night a lengthy stream of sounds reached my ears as I wrestled with my school studies. There were equally long silences when I thought she had finished. Eventually I realised she was having a conversation with her Heavenly Father. My guess is that its substance was far richer and deeper than anything in this little collection of meditations. The best I can hope for is that the lightness of touch in the imaginary conversations that follow attempts to convey her gentle sense of humour. Perhaps you'll smile more at the prayers than anything else – which is another subject, for another day.

As for the exact form of the prayers: once again I turned to George Herbert. In his poem *The Collar*, we find the words "My Lord" and "Child":

> *But as I raved and grew more fierce and wild*
> > *At every word,*
> *Methought I heard one calling,* Child!
> > *And I replied* My Lord.

Of course he left it at that, and it has already been said that I have rushed in where angels fear to tread. If so, please ignore the substance of the prayers, pause at this point of each meditation, and stay with your own thoughts, reflections, or silent contemplation.

When I began to write this introduction at home in London I little dreamt that the book itself would not be completed until over twenty years later, and that I would have travelled to every continent, exploring the Scriptures together with men and women, boys and girls in a rich variety of cultures and settings. I am sitting now in Penang, having last visited this section in Gwynedd, North Wales, after returning from India, Kenya, Uganda, Finland, Cambodia and Malaysia. Hopefully the end product, though so patently interim and unfinished, is the better for the light cast on it by so many different perspectives.

Talking of India reminds me that for forty years I had been sensing that one day I would go to Maharashtra because as a boy I believed God had called me there. When I eventually arrived in 1997 I knew immediately that this period of meantime, gestation, was part of a much wider purpose, even a plan. In my case I can now look back and see that it was a time of necessary preparation. And so, as it happened, the forty-year, forty-day biblical pattern of meantime had become true in my own life, and slowly everything has fallen into place and made sense. But in a lifetime, forty years is quite a big meantime or parenthesis!

Part 1 LOOKING BACK

THE "MEANTIME", with ordinary rhythms and activities, is sometimes too busy or fraught for reflection, sometimes too demanding or routine. But there are constant reminders that time is passing, and it has not always been ordinary, not always the same. If it is now summer, then there was a winter with memories of frost, snow, of huddles around the fire. If it is now a life full of activity and work, there was a previous life-stage, perhaps childhood with its endless holidays and summer evenings. If life is now lived alone, there were those shared times in family and at school. The ordinary is set in a context, and often that context will go back to previous generations, perhaps even previous eras, to moments of achievement, solidarity or tragedy. There can be no sense of present identity without history and this is as true for the individual as it is for any group.

Of course, looking back may be an escape or regression from the present. It can create an ideal, mythical past, a golden age. But it can also provide bearings, perspectives on the present; it can provide roots to identity and the key to the meaning of current patterns and traditions. The present, however ordinary, will have been shaped by the past – buildings perhaps, manners, mealtimes, shopping conventions, buildings, annual events. If the meantime is seen as a period between "events", then it exists because of an awareness of what was, as well as hopes or fears of what might be.

Whether we take them or not, the meantime may provide unique opportunities for reflection. In the excitement of special events and celebrations we are caught up in meeting, planning and enjoyment of the present. It is when we have time that the conversation turns to the past, when photos are taken out and shared, when thoughts can range back to early memories and experiences. The meantime is perhaps most perfectly represented by those times around the embers of a fire, when we linger and chat for no other reason than that the fire has not yet gone out and there is nothing pressing to do!

Without this process the past is either lost completely or acts unconsciously on the present, shaping behaviour and patterns irrespective of present needs and aspirations. Without the meantime we would be caught up in a succession of happenings. Perhaps modern life, with its emphasis on instant information and increasing "efficiency", is geared to squeezing out the meantime so that we cannot recreate the past or integrate its lessons into our lives and plans. The historian Eric Hobsbawm believed that loss of memory is a particular feature of contemporary societies: "The destruction of the past, or rather of the social mechanisms that link one's contemporary experience to that of earlier generations, is one of the most characteristic and eerie phenomena of the late twentieth century." (E. Hobsbawm, *Age of Extremes*, London: Abacus, 1994, page 3)

If it is true a person or group with no past has no future, then this is serious indeed. The fact is, of course, that every person, every group, does have a history: what is needed is the reflection on and understanding of that history. It is possible to regress into the past as a haven sheltering us from present realities; it is also possible to dig into the past rather like a process of personal and emotional mining. Much will be ordinary but there will be the occasional gems ... and at times possibly what may seem more like unexploded bombs.

Human beings and social organisations alone in creation can transcend the present in such a way. But to do so effectively we need those with long memories and experience in order to remain in touch with the route we have travelled, directly or indirectly.

1. Remembering

"When you enter the land that the LORD will give you as he promised, observe this ceremony. And when your children ask you, 'What does this ceremony mean to you?' then tell them, 'It is the Passover sacrifice to the LORD, who passed over the houses of the Israelites in Egypt and spared our homes when he struck down the Egyptians.'"
EXODUS 12:25-27

"Remember the days of old; consider the generations long past. Ask your father and he will tell you, your elders, and they will explain to you."
DEUTERONOMY 32:7

STILL TODAY Jewish Passover celebration involves the question from the youngest child to the older generation. I have had the privilege of taking part in a Passover with a Jewish family and recall the pride and joy on the radiant face of the little girl who asked the special question on that particular occasion.

Although the Passover recalls but one of the great events in the story of the people of Israel, it has a pre-eminent place and infuses all other celebrations. The Bible teems with memories of the stories of the people of Israel in Egypt, coming out of Egypt, crossing the Red Sea. There are speeches, poems, hymns, stories, festivals, processions, repeated over and over again. The advice of Deuteronomy 32 (above) is taken to heart in Jewish life and worship. Why? Because Passover recalls and embodies how the nation began, and where it all started. Moses (and after him Joshua, and religious leaders of Israel) recognised the value of fixing special events in the collective and individual memories of his people. Not only did those that were with him have objects to associate with happenings and experiences (tablets of stone, the Ark of the Covenant, meals) but the ground was prepared for future generations.

In the process of remembering history is not only introduced to the minds of the next generation: it also helps to bring it alive again, bring it together, in the lives of the older generation. The roots of the word "remember" remind us that it is in essence: re-membering. That is, putting things back together, making them whole in our individual mind or in community.

It is hard to find contemporary equivalents of Passover in Christian worship where individuals, families, different generations, the gathered worshipping community and the society as a whole, all remember at the same time and event. Christmas is perhaps the nearest. This is the most loved festival in our family year.

But we have chosen to incorporate the same child's Passover question into our annual Founders' Day celebration at Mill Grove, the community where I live. Every November 20th as we sit down to our birthday meal a younger member of the family asks one of the older members of the family what it means. The story of the coming of little motherless Rosie into the care of Herbert White and Ma Hutchin in 1899, while Queen Victoria was still on the throne, is recounted each year. And slowly the origins of this community become part of the collective memory and meaning of a new generation.

There are of course many ways in which the process of remembering is triggered apart from direct questions like this. Everyday life, however simple and regular, is brimful of reminders of things past. A chair, a piece of clothing, a scent or smell, food, some music, dust in a sunbeam, birdsong, a sunset touch, will stir or trigger thoughts. For an elderly woman a photo may bring back days of beauty and attraction. There may be pictures, ornaments, books that have a special meaning. In this way time past is always present, whether in the mind of an individual or a group. As I have been putting these thoughts together I have been reading that huge work of Marcel Proust, *A la Recherche du Temps Perdu*. Anyone who has delved into it knows how persistently and deeply Proust explores exactly this theme. Past and present are in constant interplay, and through the imagination the past is retained, recreated, re-membered and therefore living.

Instinctively we all find ways of remembering the past. When we go to a museum, to an historic event or special place we often come back with souvenirs. They are literally "things of remembrance". Then there are holiday photographs, family albums, a family Bible, diaries and letters, memoirs, keepsakes, anniversaries. These are all aids to the memory: helping us to hold the past in our consciousness.

And in the lives of families and churches every act of worship is an act of remembrance whether conscious or unconscious. Worship by its nature recalls and builds on the past: the creation of the world, the call of Abraham, the crossing of the Red Sea, the bravery of David, the wisdom of Solomon, the life of Christ, his death and resurrection. Regular services such as baptism and communion, as well as special festivals like Easter and Christmas, all gather up and recreate the past dramatically. As soon as music and language are introduced into a service they begin to build bridges with bygone ages and people long-since departed. Language is living, but it is not something we invent as we learn it: rather we inherit it, and its roots go back generations and across continents. The way we think, the way we categorise, is shaped by things past.

The remembering and experiencing of God's saving acts is the life-blood of the church and the people of Israel. (This image is, of course, of profound significance in both the Jewish and Christian faiths.) The same is true of the individual Christian. The place of testimonies and ceremonies (dedication, baptism, church membership, confirmation) is crucial. Luther on occasion had great bouts of depression, doubt and despair. It was during such crises that the fact of his baptism was so important. When Jesus was tempted he instinctively turned for help to the

Scriptures, the record of God's dealings with Israel: through memorising them they had become part of his life.

One of my annual responsibilities at Mill Grove is to collate a record of events which is sent to the worldwide family in a newsletter we call *Links*. It is a task that I look forward to each January. Photos, diaries, programmes, cards, letters, are all collected and then laid out together as a basis for what is selected. Without fail I am surprised, and sometimes overwhelmed, when I begin to recall all that has happened in the previous twelve months. We live by faith and every event or evidence of growth is in its way a testimony to God's care and love. The well-known chorus, though it may sound trite to some, has got it right:

> *"Count your blessings; name them one by one*
> *And it will surprise you what the Lord has done."*

For every person, as for every community, there should always be a place in the meantime for remembering. It is one of the ways we keep in touch with our own roots and identity, and in the process our experience of God is brought to mind. Thus the past can infuse the present. Sometimes memories will be part of the process which nourishes us and keeps us going. We draw on them as a personal reservoir; as we grow older that reservoir grows. If all lives were flux and excitement, full of revolution and change, then there would be little chance of remembering. It is the ordinariness of the many silent weeks, months and years, with their predictability and mechanised routine, which provides space for remembering. There are usually memories to treasure, however hard or painful life has been. But the potential for remembering in the meantime is not always realised.

As an example there are some children whose lives have been so disrupted and broken that their conscious memories ("life-stories") have been completely interrupted. Perhaps there has been no consistent adult with whom to reflect upon and interpret the past, and with whom they can share their recollections; photos and records may be totally absent. Perhaps the past has been so painful that unconscious forces have repressed it. There was an occasion, at which I was present, when members of a family of several children were discussing their early years. The eldest, a boy, could not remember a single thing in one period of over two years, whether it related to home, school, himself or others. It subsequently became clear that this was a period following his mother's death and involved excruciating events and memories. They were too painful for him to bear. Unconsciously the past was so painfully present it was too much for his consciousness to cope with. So it had been "frozen".

Thankfully this is an exceptional (though not uncommon) story, but for all of us repressed memories will, over time, need to be allowed to surface and be shared if we are to experience well-being, wholeness or re-membering. Two of the most helpful catalysts in this process are patterns of family life and corporate acts of worship. Where they are healthy we will find time and space to explore the past: shared and individual memories together. It is all too easy for the minister, as for us, to be so bound up in doing and planning that little time and space is given for quiet meditation and reflection on things past.

PRAYERS

"Lord,
On reflection I realise I probably haven't paused sufficiently to remember things past. Forgive me for those times when business, anxiety or painful associations have pushed memories aside. One consequence, sadly, is that I rarely recall and thank you for all you have done in my life. I am not sure how to go about it, but I would like a pattern of life and worship to develop in my personal and corporate life that allows time for reflection on your steadfast love."

"Child,
You've already taken your first, faltering step, but don't underestimate how difficult it is to make space for remembering. A culture of "24/7" information flows and

communication isn't good for this. Could you make some regular space in your diary right away? By the way, how do your church, family or organisation reflect on the past week, or year?"

2. Thanking

Give thanks to the LORD, for he is good;
his love endures for ever.
Let the redeemed of the LORD say this –
those he redeemed from the hand of the foe,
those he gathered from the lands,
from east and west, from north and south.

Let them give thanks to the LORD for his unfailing love
and his wonderful deeds for men.
Let them sacrifice thank-offerings
and tell of his works with songs of joy.
PSALM 107:1-3,21-22

Now on his way to Jerusalem, Jesus travelled along the border between
Samaria and Galilee. As he was going into a village, ten men who had
leprosy met him. They stood at a distance and called out in a loud voice,
"Jesus, Master, have pity on us!" When he saw them, he said, "Go, show
yourselves to the priests." And as they went, they were cleansed. One of
them, when he saw he was healed, came back, praising God in a loud
voice. He threw himself at Jesus' feet and thanked him – and he was a
Samaritan. Jesus asked, "Were not all ten cleansed? Where are the other
nine? Was no-one found to return and give praise to God except this

foreigner?" Then he said to him, "Rise and go; your faith has made you well."

LUKE 17:11-19

I F YOU HAVE a Bible to hand, you will discover that the first part of Psalm 107 (verses 1-21) describes three desperate human situations in which people cry out to God and then he responds to their cries. They are asylum seekers, prisoners and outcasts. In turn the Psalmist implores such people to give thanks to the Lord. Once we start to think symbolically, we realise that they include you and I. The incident from Luke's life of Jesus embodies aspects of all three situations in a poignant way, for a leper was wholly cut off (cast out) from ordinary social life. Both passages give a central place to "thanksgiving" (tellingly the word seems almost old-fashioned and stilted), which is usually associated with festivals: for example "Thanksgiving Day" in the USA and Harvest Thanksgiving in the UK.

One way of describing the ordinary life of faith of the believer or a follower of Jesus would be to call it a continuous response to God's love: it is a personal "Thank you". The more we reflect on what God has done, the more we want to thank him for his grace. One of the biblical words for thank is "praise". That key unlocks the door to an understanding of how much we are encouraged to thank God in the Scriptures: thanksgiving and praise permeate the whole of the Bible.

In normal family life there are usually a few good-mannered "thank-yous", whether at home, at work or shopping. These are usually said out of habit. Meanwhile much is just taken for granted. Compared to what they are and do mothers are probably the most under-thanked people on earth. At Mill Grove we find youngsters make our home so much theirs that they come to accept all the benefits as their natural right. In a sense that's a great compliment. Yet we so often find that later on in life there is a dawning awareness of just how much they accepted without thinking: how much they took for granted. It can be 50 or 60 years before something sets off a desire to say "Thank you".

It makes a significant difference when an activity or action is seen not just as self-contained but as connected to what has gone before and part of a response to what God has done. Some of the great artists, poets and writers are responding to what they recognise as God's creation and his gifts. Their work is imbued with a sense of praise and gratitude. It's not a superficial thing (the words "Thank you") but a whole attitude and worldview: "What shall I render to the Lord for all his benefits?" It's not about being nostalgic and grateful, as a way of forgetting problems and pain. It's a quality of life and art.

To me this takes us near the heart of Bach's music. He is always aware that the greater Glory (or thanks) should go to God ("*ad majorem Dei gloriam*"). A sense of thankfulness may be the quality that encourages the listener to respond. It's something to do with the recognition that before Bach, God made music (and mathematics) possible. God gave prodigious gifts to Bach, and his music is a continuous act of thanks. Any talent ultimately derives from God and, if rightly used, will bring him worship and praise. When he accepted his Nobel Prize, Solzhenitsyn made a similar distinction between a believing and non-believing writer.

We usually associate thank-yous with presents, or with a response to an act of kindness. It would involve a revolution in attitude, or a paradigm-shift, to be thankful for those things, people, events that have caused us difficulty or pain, distress or humiliation. Yet that is where the great prophets and followers of Jesus have gone before us. Peter and the apostles were thankful they had been counted worthy to suffer a beating for Jesus, and Paul likewise rejoices because he has entered so fully into the life (and sufferings) of his master. It's not that people were asking for pain, but that they came to see in it a way of identifying with Jesus, the one they followed, and who had been there before them. They also sought to understand God's meaning and purpose in and through every aspect of life.

Mary Craig called her book, about a child born with a disability, *Blessings*; Mark and Caroline called their first daughter, born with Down's syndrome, Elizabeth Joy. These were acts of faith, recognising that never having asked for such children, they had come to accept them, and to learn from them and from their relationships, that God could be thanked.

They had brought extra blessings in and through the heart-searching and agony. In some way they were more complete as a result of their experiences. Thanking is a way of embracing a person or situation.

There has been a school for children with cerebral palsy at Mill Grove for many years, and as I have got to know the parents of the children, this has been a common refrain. They have been granted insights into the heart of things that are hidden from many others. When I led the funeral and thanksgiving service (yes, that's exactly what it was called) for one of the young people who had died in his teens, the sense of shared understanding and empathy between those who knew what his family was going through was palpable.

A simple function of ordinary work is to earn a living to fund a lifestyle or family. As we recognise that health and strength are essential to perform any work, it can mean that the very act of working is an expression of thankfulness. A life of thankfulness takes nothing for granted. All life is God-given, and God is to be praised.

There are those who have a real gift or ministry of thanks: who always have a creative way of saying "Thank you" and the regular exercise of that ministry brings so much joy. Everyone remembers to say "Thank you" for special events or presents. It takes real sensitivity to thank the milkman, the postman, our work colleagues (especially our juniors), our husband or wife, parents or children, day in and day out. Seen in this light there is always someone to thank or something for which to say "Thank you".

I used to play a very occasional, and very amateur, round of golf. It was a source of relaxation: not only hitting the ball in good company, but being on the hills of Hainault Forest accompanied by rabbits, foxes, magpies, woodpeckers, blue-tits, rosebay willow-herb, oak trees, and overlooking the great Thames Basin, with occasional glimpses of Canary Wharf. It provided a rounded experience in itself. But there was something more to it: I have a fine set of clubs and they were given me by a dear late friend, a Scottish chemist, who played golf better than I ever will, but whose heart condition meant he could play no more. Before he died he called me to his house and passed his set on to me. He even gave me some free coaching on my wedge shots!

So for me every round of golf has been a way of saying "Thank you" to him for his gift. It was never for me about tournaments and excellence. At heart I'm just thankful I can play golf at all. In a sense every shot is a thank-you to Jock.

Perhaps there are hidden, gentle, constant parallels in your life which are like parables of the Christian's relationship with his or her Saviour and Lord, and which are unconscious acts of thanks. They look back, without remembering, to the author and source of all things.

Living in a city like London provides the opportunity to study hundreds of human faces on buses, trains and in the streets. Faces record a great deal of a person's life story and character: the older they become, the more it is etched into lines, lips, brow and eyes. Some reveal a sense of struggle, others of fear, bitterness, pride, resignation. But some faces are open, relaxed, and seem to me to reflect a life of thankfulness. They radiate a quiet attitude of praise and acceptance of grace. I have never enquired of the owners of these varieties of face what they might tell me of their stories, but looking back with or without thankfulness will over time result in totally different personalities, revealed quite unconsciously by the face.

The meantime is a time when we may not be able to see or even plan the very next step ahead, but it does afford us opportunities to look back and be thankful to the One "who from our mothers' arms has blessed us on our way".

PRAYERS

"Lord,
  At heart I suppose I'm more like the nine people Jesus healed
  who didn't come back to thank him than the one who did. I get
  uptight about others who take your name in vain while I now
  realise that at the same time I tend to take your gifts for
  granted. Help me to respond gratefully to each new day, each
  new task, each person in such a way that even if no one else sees,
  you know that I really want to thank you, Lord. I'm not a Bach,

Solzhenitsyn or Jack Nicklaus, but I want to use my limited
gifts to express my gratitude. I'll leave my fate to you!"

"Child,
Whatever you do, please don't stop taking me for granted! I'm
always there. You don't have to worry for one moment about
that. And please don't try to be conscious of me all the time
either, trying to remember to say the words 'Thank you' all the
time. As you enter into a task or relationship do it to the very
best of your ability, and without thinking of me. If it is good,
you will find it is a way of praising me. Corporate praise gathers
up much that goes unnoticed by others."

3. Repaying

How can I repay the LORD
 for all his goodness to me?
I will lift up the cup of salvation
 and call on the name of the LORD.
I will fulfil my vows to the LORD
 in the presence of all his people.

Precious in the sight of the LORD
 is the death of his saints.
O LORD, truly I am your servant;
 I am your servant, the son of your maidservant;
 you have freed me from my chains.

I will sacrifice a thank-offering to you
 and call on the name of the LORD.
I will fulfil my vows to the LORD
 in the presence of all his people,
in the courts of the house of the LORD –
 in your midst, O Jerusalem.

Praise the LORD.
PSALM 116:12-19

Jesus entered Jericho and was passing through. A man was there by the name of Zacchaeus; he was a chief tax collector and was wealthy. He wanted to see who Jesus was, but being a short man he could not, because of the crowd. So he ran ahead and climbed a sycamore-fig tree to see him, since Jesus was coming that way.

When Jesus reached the spot, he looked up and said to him, "Zacchaeus, come down immediately. I must stay at your house today." So he came down at once and welcomed him gladly.

All the people saw this and began to mutter, "He has gone to be the guest of a 'sinner'."

But Zacchaeus stood up and said to the Lord, "Look, Lord! Here and now I give half of my possessions to the poor, and if I have cheated anybody out of anything, I will pay back four times the amount."

Jesus said to him, "Today salvation has come to this house, because this man, too, is a son of Abraham. For the Son of Man came to seek and to save what was lost."

LUKE 19:1-10

B OTH THE WRITER of Psalm 116 and Zacchaeus the tax collector experienced God's intervention in their lives. The Psalmist felt that life itself was slipping from him and called out in desperation "O Lord, save me!" See the first part of the psalm, especially verse 4. Zacchaeus found Jesus choosing to enter his home (of all places!) and shine the light of truth on his past dealings. Looking back they both felt that repayment should be made. The Psalmist saw this as an act of re-dedication to God in worship; Zacchaeus knew he must put right wrongful dealings with those from whom he had taken too much tax. They both knew they were in God's debt because of his saving acts.

For many individuals, families, organisations and nations, daily life literally revolves around the struggle to repay debts. Time will tell whether the "global debt crisis" of the early twenty-first century is here to stay. For some there is the mortgage, month by month for periods of twenty to twenty-five years. For others there is rent. For many there is the repayment of goods purchased through hire purchase agreements: presents for Christmas or birthdays, clothes or furnishings for the home.

There are other types of repayment which involve no direct use of money. When children care for their elderly parents it is, consciously or not, a repayment of years of care and support decades earlier. In practice it is most often a single female caring for a mother or father for years of her life. In work, business and organisations there is an "informal economy" where people will do favours for each other in response to favours done in the past. It is probable that social life would founder without such reciprocal processes.

As a former alumnus, I regularly receive a magazine from the University of Oxford, and my college. They contain interesting updates, but the stated intention is to elicit gifts from me. But, why me? Do they really know how lacking in disposable income I am? The reason Oxford asks me is because I have benefited from three years among the ivory towers – one of them in a room just above the "Bridge of Sighs" joining the two quads of Hertford College. And they know I am so grateful for the incomparable all-round education I received.

When someone dies there are, of course, tributes and flowers. A tradition has grown up in some countries of monetary donations for a cause nominated by the deceased person or their family. Quite often this cause is the organisation that has been caring for the person or tackling the illness from which they suffered. It is a repayment. Many charities target advertising on just this sector, because it is such a significant trend. At Mill Grove we make no appeals for funds or donations, and so it is interesting to see how people sometimes choose to give to us in memory of a loved one who has died. There is usually reference in accompanying letters to "how much the person meant to me".

Processes of repayment can therefore be conscious or unconscious, direct and indirect. They may be chosen responses of joy or demanded responses which are crippling. Some years ago one of our Mill Grove family got into massive debt (without our knowing about it). It opened our eyes to the loneliness and hopelessness of the debtor. Repayments seemed like digging a hole in a sand dune – the harder you dig, the more sand falls into the hole. The shadow of repayment may be cast over the rest of his life. It is this that has opened our eyes to the wretched realities of whole communities and nations in similar predicaments.

Christians and Jews alike are people who see themselves as indebted to God. The Jews were redeemed from slavery ("bought out of" slavery) and Christians have received God's free gift of salvation which was bought with a price. Much New Testament writing and hymnology reflects on our indebtedness to God. He has given everything in and through Jesus to "pay the price of sin". Significantly this unequal relationship is never seen in Scripture as something that is crippling or enslaving. And we need to ponder this. How can it be that we should be in such great debt without it overshadowing and oppressing our lives like a cloud?

The Psalmist and Zacchaeus demonstrate the truth that the repayment of debt to God is not a grim and relentless duty enforced upon them. It is not a demand notice: there is no hint of the shadow or the footsteps of the bailiff! Their desire to repay springs from another source and other motives deep within them. You can feel the lightness of touch, the sense of release and joy as you read their thoughts.

The reason is surely that the relationship is not based on gain or repayment but on love. It is an honour, a privilege to be the one on whom God showers his love. Repayment is a joy and in that repayment we find joy and purpose. It leads to fulfilment, not captivity. For the indebtedness derives from a cancellation of a debt, and with this comes a transformed relationship. Our very status has changed so much we are in effect a new creation. The repayment is also an amazing declaration of trust. Our God has "invested" everything in us: lavished his love upon us. Like a pupil of a chess grandmaster, every time we play we are repaying our debt, but that is not why we play – we play because we enjoy the game of chess. In the same way Christians live to express our love for God, with the gifts he has given.

Sadly, much religious activity seems to be motivated by fear and duty. It is almost as if God is seen as a sort of spiritual moneylender anxious to safeguard and maximise his returns. There is little sense of spontaneity or joy in worship – merely a weekly or yearly routine not unlike the trip to repay those to whom money is owed. If we sense any hint of this in our own experience, it needs to be brought out into the open. Why a feeling of duty? Who has shaped the experience? Is there any indication of why the "price paid" by Jesus is seen to be incomplete or crippling. The meantime may afford us sustained opportunities to look back and ponder the extent and quality of God's love. If so the very idea of repayment will take on a wholly new hue.

Before praying the prayers below why not take another glance at the psalm? This is the essence of true worship and our relationship with God.

PRAYERS

"Lord,
It's only as I reflect on all your goodness to me in everyday life that I realise how much I am in your debt. I recognise that it is a lavish love-gift that motivates all your actions. Will you accept my daily actions and my weekly offerings, willingly and joyfully given, O God, my strength and my redeemer? And will you help me to be free of any sense of resentment, fear and drudgery in your service?"

"Child,
Let's not worry about how much we love or give to each other. Perhaps you could pray for and help those, deep in debt and trapped in crippling structures and relationships. Freely you have received, freely give."

4. Fasting

"Is not this the kind of fasting I have chosen:
to loose the chains of injustice
and untie the cords of the yoke,
to set the oppressed free
and break every yoke?
Is it not to share your food with the hungry
and to provide the poor wanderer with shelter;
when you see the naked, to clothe him,
and not to turn away from your own flesh and blood?"
ISAIAH 58:6-7

On the first day Jonah started into the city. He proclaimed: "Forty more
days and Nineveh will be overturned." The Ninevites believed God.
They declared a fast, and all of them, from the greatest to the least, put
on sackcloth.
JONAH 3:4-5

Jesus, full of the Holy Spirit, returned from the Jordan and was led by
the spirit in the desert, where for forty days he was tempted by the devil.
He ate nothing during those days, and at the end of them he was hungry.
LUKE 4:1-2

FASTING IS a very concrete example of the "meantime of life": it exists in the space between meals. A previous meal is being digested, and there will be the next one. Every night's sleep is a limited but real type of fasting, as the English word "breakfast" reminds us. Strictly speaking fasting can be a period of contemplation (being in the present) or preparation (for future ministry of activity), as well as a means of looking back. By locating this reflection in this section of the book we are dealing with only one of these aspects. There is much more that could be said from these other perspectives and in other contexts.

A common reason, or motive, for fasting is an acknowledgement of sin and the acceptance of responsibility for it. This is why the great city of Nineveh fasted. Jonah is indignant at God's refusal to judge the city because he, like its inhabitants, reckons the collective sins to be so grievous. When there is this awareness of sin and guilt it simply isn't possible to carry on life as normal. Fasting is an immediate and concrete way of taking stock and giving space and time to a reflection on the past.

Another example is when Ezra read from the Book of the Law to the exiles who had gathered in Jerusalem (Nehemiah 8 and 9). The people fasted as a sign of their acceptance of the sin of their nation past and present. It was a corporate act of confession and repentance without parallel in the Scriptures. As each section of the Law was read it became clear how much they had deviated from God's way like lost sheep. Fasting was not only an opportunity for such reflection but a self-inflicted punishment for that wrong-doing.

The fasting of Jesus in the wilderness is a prelude to, or preparation for, his ministry. It can, in short, be treated as something forward-looking. Certainly it is not a confession of sin or a punishment for sin and wrongdoing. Yet it is a looking back in at least two respects. First, in a very neat way it gathers up a period of Jewish history and so continues the identification of Jesus, the Messiah, with his people. Having been in Egypt as a child, he later spends forty days in the wilderness. The special founding period and experiences of his people are thus recreated and relived in his own person. Second, the dialogue (or argument) with the Tempter also looks back (as well as forward) to how he understands his calling in the light of the purposes of God revealed in the Scriptures. We should not underestimate the intensity of the challenge: "If you are the Son of God ..." as it hearkens back to the words of his Father at the baptism. Both Jesus and Satan quote the Scriptures and the period of fasting gives space for meditation on the words God has given to his people.

The Jewish Sabbath from sundown to sundown is sometimes observed with fasting, and some form of fasting plays a part in the regular pattern of all other major world religions. It is associated with a discipline involving self-denial: a way of expressing single-mindedness, solidarity with others and commitment. It symbolises the truth that we do not live by bread alone, and that our lives serve a higher purpose than the merely material. The period of Lent, patterned on the forty days Jesus spent in the wilderness and leading up to Easter, is often accompanied by some form of abstinence from food or drink. Thus both Jews and Christians continue to look back to remind themselves of their identity in the light of their origins.

These are planned patterns of fasting where individuals and groups are provided with cultural norms. It is also true that loss of appetite is one of the effects of guilt, grief, bereavement, anxiety or fear. The publicity given to anorexia nervosa now reminds us of the link between abstinence from food and personal trauma and feelings of remorse or regret. The recognition given to this at the funeral in 1997 of Diana, Princess of Wales was one of the ways her struggles resonated with others. This is not fasting in the sense we understand it, but a poignant reminder of the inner dynamics of which fasting is an outward expression. Fasting, and reflection on the past, are inextricably linked – unconsciously, if not consciously.

In some ways there is no choice for the anorexic; but the decision not to eat is precisely about control, and the presence of food gives meaning to the decision not to eat. Sadly, there are millions in the world for whom the absence of eating is a tragic consequence of human sin and wrongdoing. It would be ostrich-like to meditate on fasting without acknowledging this sad plight of so many fellow human beings. There is acute pain as I write these words among the street children of Mumbai.

For those of us who have a choice there may be a decision at certain times to engage in formal (recognised) fasting along with others of our faith. On the other hand the Bible encourages us to apply the principles of fasting to everyday life. This is the teaching of Isaiah in that great chapter, 58, which should be read before praying the prayer below. It opens up a whole new dimension to fasting that is so challenging that it should be read only after a health warning! The call is not to look inwardly, to do as it were a spiritual health check, but rather to change the whole orientation of our lives, so that we serve God's purposes in everyday life with particular reference to the injustice that blights the lives of so many with whom we share the planet. Injustice is not something abstract: we are always involved on one side of the struggle. Fasting is the call to recognise that God is on the side of the oppressed and to reshape our priorities and lives in order to be alongside him in his righteous acts.

It was Luther who said that lay Christians should be monks in every aspect of life: the whole of life should be a monastery – given over to living according to God's rule. And fasting is part of that process. It may mean more disciplined living and use of time. It may be that we understand better the enforced fasting that has followed trauma or wrongdoing in our own lives. We should never seek to draw attention to whatever our decided course of action is. In the process we shall be joining a great band of those who have gone before and who recognise that the closer they grow to their Lord and Saviour the more they realise their own sin and frailty.

Fasting can be seen as an aspect of a wilderness experience, and we cannot develop in the Christian faith without it, whatever the actual form it may take. In a very apt way it represents the truth, already noted, that we live between the "Now" and the "Not Yet" of the kingdom. For many Christians in Lent this means looking back to Shrove Tuesday and the anticipation of Easter Day. The Christian who never fasts is out of touch – with Christian life and worship, with the reality of suffering of many in our world, with the nature of the kingdom of God, and with the life of the Lord Jesus Christ.

If we are to be *in* Christ, in his death and resurrection, so we should be with him, as it were, in the desert. Mealtimes are part of ordinary life; for many they are social occasions, times of meeting and sharing. We also need those times when we are alone, our minds and bodies focused on God's presence and will. Just as we sleep each night, so fasting, however limited and specific, is a natural part of our walk with our Saviour. Lent is then a microcosm of the Christian life, not an exception.

PRAYERS

"Lord,
This connects with a very real longing quite deep within me to serve you, follow you and love you by identifying with you in every respect. At the same time I constantly find there are tides in everyday life that counteract the winds of your Spirit. You know I want to fast in Isaiah's daunting sense. You know I try. It seems easier and more manageable in the symbolic acts of Lent than in the whole of life. Is that any good, I wonder?"

"Child,
Never underestimate the symbolic acts of prayer and fasting: they have their place. But if you are ready to make an act of will to identify with your Saviour, strive for a daily or weekly pattern. You will probably need to do this alongside others who are also committed to disciplined living, in order to help each other. This will be of more use than a yearly token. You will notice the daily pattern of Jesus if you look at the Gospels carefully enough."

5. Celebrating

Hezekiah sent word to all Israel and Judah, and also wrote letters to Ephraim and Manasseh, inviting them to come to the temple of the LORD in Jerusalem and celebrate the Passover to the LORD, the God of Israel. The king and his officials and the whole assembly in Jerusalem decided to celebrate the Passover in the second month. They had not been able to celebrate it at the regular time because not enough priests had consecrated themselves and the people had not assembled in Jerusalem. The plan seemed right both to the king and to the whole assembly. They decided to send a proclamation throughout Israel, from Beersheba to Dan, calling the people to come to Jerusalem and celebrate the Passover to the LORD, the God of Israel. It had not been celebrated in large numbers according to what was written.

The Israelites who were present in Jerusalem celebrated the Feast of Unleavened Bread for seven days with great rejoicing, while the Levites and priests sang to the LORD every day, accompanied by the LORD's instruments of praise.

2 CHRONICLES 30:1-5,21

"But while he was still a long way off, his father saw him and was filled with compassion for him. He ran to his son, threw his arms around him and kissed him.

"The son said to him, 'Father, I have sinned against heaven and against you. I am no longer worthy to be called your son.' But the father said to his servants, 'Quick! Bring the best robe and put it on him. Put a ring on his finger and sandals on his feet. Bring the fattened calf and kill it. Let's have a feast and celebrate. For this son of mine was dead and is alive again; he was lost and is found.' So they began to celebrate.

"Meanwhile, the older son was in the field. When he came near the house, he heard music and dancing. So he called one of the servants and asked him what was going on. 'Your brother has come,' he replied, 'and your father has killed the fattened calf because he has him back safe and sound.' The older brother became angry and refused to go in. So his father went out and pleaded with him. But he answered his father, 'Look! All these years I've been slaving for you and never disobeyed your orders. Yet you never gave me even a young goat so I could celebrate with my friends. But when this son of yours who has squandered your property with prostitutes comes home, you kill the fattened calf for him!'

"'My son,' the father said, 'you are always with me, and everything I have is yours. But we had to celebrate and be glad, because this brother of yours was dead and is alive again; he was lost and is found.'"

LUKE 15:20-32

THE CELEBRATION of Hezekiah is one of the great acts of worship in the Scriptures, ranking alongside the dedication of the Temple of Solomon and the rebuilding of Jerusalem (Ezra and Nehemiah). Most British celebrations seem short and reserved compared to the seven days described in 2 Chronicles. The Queen's Diamond Jubilee in June 2012 was a notable exception that seemed to take the nation by surprise. But Israel's celebrations right down to the present day have always been of a different order. The celebration of the homecoming of the Prodigal was likely to have been in this rich and full-hearted Jewish tradition. The fact that the first miracle in John's Gospel was at a wedding feast, or celebration, should make us ponder the significance of such events.

These two celebrations are, of course, very special in the history of the people of Israel. They are among the most significant and precious moments ever described. Yet we also talk of celebrating a birthday, an anniversary or an event like the passing of a driving test, or an exam, or a victory in sport. These are more common and routine. And celebration can also be patterned into daily life. At best it becomes a dimension of living such that every action, every relationship is tinged with the joy of celebration.

Celebrating usually has an element of looking back or remembering, in that it is a reaction to something that has already happened whether in the immediate past (a wedding breakfast, a Cup Final victory), the medium term (like independence for India in 1947), or many years ago (the Passover or Christmas). Every group, every family, every nation, every religion builds regular times of celebration into its calendar – national holidays, birthdays, Sabbaths, Sundays. For ordinary life to have meaning, there has to be a way of linking with, drawing strength from, the past great moments of the group or groups of which we are a part. And celebrations are probably one of the best ways of doing this, whether we realise it or not.

So, when celebrations dwindle or cease, it may well be that the life of a group is declining or in jeopardy. They may wind down because an event in the past loses significance, or because not everyone recognises it as special. When they are enjoyed by everyone they light up the most mundane periods of existence. They can be sources of unity and inspiration in times of bewildering deprivation and isolation. The Jewish people have celebrated Sabbaths and festivals in every sort of distress, dispersal or despair. Christians have celebrated communion in prison with no bread, wine or priest available.

In more normal and less stressful times worship is a regular form of celebration. In some way the originating event or events are recreated, entered into, experienced afresh. They come alive. It's often when younger people enter into such occasions with unalloyed enthusiasm and total acceptance that the meaning flashes out. Christmas is a time which is only complete when children are present: they are essential to the full and rounded celebration. It is inherently inter-generational. I think it is for this reason that Christmas is so very special and memorable in our own residential community.

We can miss out on celebration because we are sad, depressed, busy, preoccupied, or because the event means nothing. One of the points of the story of the "Prodigal Son", so often missed in an abridged reading of it, is the fact that the older son does not celebrate. The reason is that he has never entered into the sadness of losing his brother – he doesn't seem to have missed him as a person, so when he is found again there is no reason to celebrate and be glad. In Luke's gospel three stories are grouped together – a lost sheep, a lost coin, and a lost son. They all end with a celebration. The only person in all three stories who misses out on one of those celebrations is the older brother.

And what a sad relationship he has with such a loving father! Life had obviously been nothing but a grind for him: work, work and more work. There seems to have been no joy in daily living. Properly understood every meal is a celebration, a celebration of creation; every journey is a celebration, a re-creation of our spiritual pilgrimage; every task is a celebration that we are created in God's image; every relationship is a celebration of the loving Trinity at the heart of creation; every shopping expedition is a celebration of the stewardship that is ours and our wealth compared to others. The Celtic tradition and prayers for every aspect of ordinary life can help us here.

Though few achieve it, we all know those for whom there is a joy at the heart of things. The present moment is a sacrament: experienced uniquely and joyfully in itself, but also entered into as an echo of the great saving acts of God himself. When Paul spoke of being content in all situations, he was hinting at the way in which even suffering and hardship provided means of entering more fully into the life and death and resurrection of his Lord.

It is a joy in our family at Mill Grove to have many occasions for celebration (possibly more than is fair) – football victories, a hat-trick, a first step, an exam passed, an engagement, a birth, a successful interview, progress at school resulting in a commendation, someone learning to swim, skate, ride a bike, sail or play an instrument, a special evening at a concert or drama when someone is taking part, and friends who are enjoying all these things.

But it is not the moments themselves so much as the space in between where the dance of celebration is. The smile as a face lights up on meeting another; the shared humour recalling things past and understood; the meal which is so lovingly prepared it makes simple fare become a banquet. The most joyful celebratory meal I ever had consisted of nothing but cabbage! It was in the home of a Russian artist to whom we had just brought tubes of titanium white paint for which he had been waiting for months. His wife created a masterpiece out of the most basic of vegetables.

With this attitude in which every aspect of an event is noticed and appreciated, the life of Jesus was a continuous act of celebration. Others were bowled over by a particular miracle or event, but for him the celebration was continuous. If we, like him, were as close to our Creator God in everyday things our lives would be acts of celebration. We can, of course, see routine as dull. We repeat things over and over again. But if seen as if for the first time each day, each sky, each flower, each person we encounter is a ground for celebration.

Perhaps that's why children are particularly good at celebrating: they are experiencing so much for the very first time. Is this what Jesus was referring to among other things when he talked of the things that are hidden from the wise and learned and revealed to little children? Do children see things as if at the dawn of creation, fresh and newly experienced each day?

PRAYERS

"Lord,
Is genuine celebration becoming less common and less real in today's world? Perhaps it's my own soul that needs to respond afresh to the echoes of joy in your heart. Forgive me for those times I have resembled the older brother and come between

you and real joyful celebration. I need your help if I am to turn my whole life into a form of worship ... what a long way I have to go!"

"Child,
Celebration isn't like fasting – an act of will; it's about relaxing and allowing yourself to receive the feelings of others. There's plenty of opportunity for rejoicing in the most ordinary day and the most ordinary act of worship. It usually begins with someone else's joy, not your own ... especially children. Welcoming a little child in my name is one of the great acts of celebration in the Kingdom of Heaven."

6. Restoring

"In this year of Jubilee everyone is to return to his own property.

"If you sell land to one of your countrymen or buy any from him, do not take advantage of each other. You are to buy from your countryman on the basis of the number of years since the Jubilee. And he is to sell to you on the basis of the number of years left for harvesting crops. When the years are many, you are to increase the price, and when the years are few, you are to decrease the price, because what he is really selling you is the number of crops. Do not take advantage of each other, but fear your God. I am the LORD your God....

"The land must not be sold permanently because the land is mine and you are but aliens and my tenants. Throughout the country that you hold as a possession you must provide for the redemption of the land."
LEVITICUS 25:13-17,23-24

"The Spirit of the Lord is on me, because he has anointed me to preach good news to the poor. He has sent me to proclaim freedom for the prisoners and recovery of sight for the blind, to release the oppressed, to proclaim the year of the Lord's favour."
LUKE 4:18-19

IT IS NOT CLEAR whether the Jubilee year ever became part of the regular life and rhythm of the Israelites in practice. The year is probably what Isaiah and Jesus were referring to as "the year of the Lord's favour". The whole idea was that once every 49 or 50 years everything stopped, Sabbath-like, and land and houses were returned to their original inhabitants, and slaves could become free. It looks back to the time when God redeemed the Israelites from Egypt and apportioned them land in Canaan. The description of the land being divided up is given in Joshua 13:5-21.

Every generation sees some progress and get comparatively powerful and wealthy, while others in comparison become or remain weak and poor. In most societies this process means that wealth is handed on from generation to generation: so the rich tend to get richer while, conversely, or partly as a direct result, many of the poor, sadly, become poorer. The Jubilee year was designed to interrupt and correct this process. The original sharing out was deemed to be fair and so every generation would receive a fresh and equal start. Things were restored to their original state.

Much of life "in the meantime" is about restoration in this sense. That is: trying to get things back to what we know or believe to have been a better, former state or condition. We are familiar with the works of great artists (the "old masters" some are called) and marvel at their creativity, their insights, their vision, their technique. But what we see today is the work of not only their brushes and palette knives. It is also the work of generations of restorers. They have painstakingly and lovingly worked away at the canvasses clearing away layers of dirt, attending to cracks and tears. The same is true of books and manuscripts. Damage has been repaired and scribes have sought to reconstruct original texts.

On my 21st birthday I was given a copy of the *Jerusalem Bible* by my Christian friends at Hertford College, Oxford. It became a wise companion to me from that moment on. I grew to love the poetic sensitivity of psalms and prophecies, the attention to the flow of the arguments in New Testament epistles, and the adventurous vocabulary throughout. I often thought I sensed J.R.R. Tolkien's presence in the

Psalms (he was a consultant for the work!). But it wasn't long before the binding started cracking and pages began to fall out. A dear friend who worked at the British Museum rebound it. It was restored and continued for many years to accompany me, like a trusted friend.

Ordinary life is largely about one form of restoration or another. Take daily tasks like washing up, washing, mending clothes, car or T.V. repairs, getting someone in to mend a washer, replacing a light bulb. It is full of simple tasks whose purpose is to restore an object or situation to its original state. This means, of course, that someone needs to know what it was like when looking right, when sounding right, when working properly.

Then there are institutions whose purpose is to put things right – the legal profession exists because things go wrong and justice is about redressing the balance, ensuring reparation is made, restitution where possible. Whenever we say or hear "that's not fair" we are making reference to how things were, how things should be. Insurance is, too, about seeking to compensate when something goes wrong so that things are reinstated to as near their original state as possible: likewise with the health service and social work professions.

After every war, the time comes when people and institutions have to start living normally again: like walking out on the streets after months inside under curfew, shopkeepers putting glass in their windows, electric cables being laid so that the era of candlelight can be replaced with modern lighting; running public bus services. In this light, what we call peace-time is often composed of long periods of restoration – for it takes years to restore a city or nation to its pre-war state.

In recent decades there has been what Andrew Walker chose to call "restoration" movements in the church. Names like "house church", "charismatic", "renewal", "emerging", "liquid", cell, messy, and many others have been used to describe the various examples and strands of what has been happening. The basic point is that those within these groups believe that the true (or a truer) pattern for the church is to be found in the early churches described in the pre-Constantinian New Testament. Since then things have become so institutionalised and removed from the pristine, early days that a primary task of these movements is to restore the church to its former integrity and glory.

This movement is nothing new. In fact one way of seeing the history of the church worldwide is as a constant process wrestling with the tension between preserving the status quo (at whatever period), and restoring things to how they used to be (or seemed to be). Religious communities and orders, charismatic individuals like St Francis of Assisi, have sought to model ways of living that they see as closer to the Kingdom of Heaven as taught and lived by Jesus.

Reformers worldwide, some by name and others less consciously, have been re-reading the Scriptures, and critiquing the church in the light of them, with a view to living in a way that is more faithful to God's way of doing things.

The essence of the meantime is cleaning and repairing things: if we don't do the repair work, slowly things stop working, decay, wear out.

So all around us, in the meantime, whether in religious and secular contexts the task of restoring things to their former state goes on. It may not be given to many to be creators, like Paul, Rembrandt, Shakespeare, Bach, but all of us can, in one way or another, be restorers, however simple, basic or repetitive that work may be.

PRAYERS

"Lord,
I'm so thankful for all those who have worked long and hard to restore the many creative works that we can enjoy. But I think I have underestimated the integral part restoration has in everyday life. There's plenty of restoration to do in my life for a start! I ask that especially in my relationships and daily life anything warped, disjointed or worn may be made new. In asking this I hope I am not underestimating the size of the task."

"Child,

How easily the precious image I planted in humankind becomes disfigured, distorted, encrusted and cracked. If you will be a restorer, day by day, beginning always with yourself rather than others or things, that is a precious role dear to my heart and purposes. I love nothing more than to lead you to green pastures and still waters where I can restore your soul. Thank you."

7. Re-creating

"So the heavens and the earth and everything in them were completed. By the seventh day God had finished the work he had been doing. So on the seventh day he rested from all his work. God blessed the seventh day and made it holy. He rested on it. After he had created everything, he rested from all the work that he had done."

GENESIS 2:1-3

"We know that all that God has created has been groaning. It is in pain as if it were giving birth to a child. The created world continues to groan even now. And that's not all. We have the Holy Spirit as the promise of future blessing. But we also groan inside ourselves as we look forward to the time when God will adopt us as full members of his family. Then he will give us everything he has for us. He will raise our bodies and give glory to them."

ROMANS 8:22-23

"Then I saw a new heaven and a new earth, for the first heaven and the first earth had passed away and there was no longer any sea. I saw the Holy City, the new Jerusalem, coming down out of heaven from God, prepared as a bride beautifully dressed for her husband."

REVELATION 21:1-2

THESE READINGS span the vast arch of time represented by the very first words of Scripture and the last; from the Creation to the New Creation. We have used the metaphor of the tides or waves of the sea to describe what "in the meantime" means. And here we have the two greatest tides or waves of all. We live, like the whole of human history, between them. And consequently we are drawn both back in wonder to the dawn of time and forward in hope to the sunrise of the age that is to come.

How do we understand, experience, and negotiate the time between these cosmic events which, properly understood, dwarf all our greatest moments, achievements and longings? It is Paul who provides one of the most enduring metaphors to describe what is going on in the meantime as a basis for establishing how we should then live. It is a metaphor of birth, or perhaps, better, rebirth. From the first Sabbath, when God rested, and what has become known as the "fall of man", a creative but painful and long drawn-out process has been going on. It is what we could call gestation or pregnancy.

Paul does not use the idea lightly. It comes in the midst of his most sustained and forthright exposition of Christian theology: the book of Romans. In it he reflects on the whole history of humankind and God's dealings with his creatures and creation. The whole of human civilization, including the greatest of creations in every art form, are compressed into, as it were, a seed, or an embryo within the womb of recorded and unrecorded history. In the process everything gains its true meaning in one thing alone: that is in the fact and way that God, the Creator is in love, re-shaping and re-making his Creation.

Nothing else ultimately matters; nothing else will last.

In an instant we see that what we took to be the unexceptional, the ordinariness, the messiness of daily life, when we cannot see things coming together or achieved, is actually how everything really is. In the mundane, the routine of life's goings out and comings in, we glimpse the true nature of all things. The self-made man; the great cities; exhibitions; treaties; world congresses; revivals; cathedrals (the list is endless) have this in common: they are part of a cosmic reshaping by God into something new.

Thus everyday life is in fact re-creation.

Strange that if this is so, we do not even use the word in common parlance! The nearest we get is "recreation": that is, leisure time or leisure pursuits or, we might even say, playing. And what do we mean by them? Basically we have in mind those times and activities which are separated from the main business and purpose of life, when we are deliberately not attempting to do anything, to achieve anything. They do not count in any record of what we have done.

It is typical of his nature that God is weaving these seemingly unconnected, disparate, trivial and marginal periods into his scheme of things. Perhaps, like Sabbath rest, they are where the real dance is? When all our strivings cease, are we possibly closer to the essence of things than when we seek to tame them, shape them, and dominate them?

What has this to do with looking back?

The book of Genesis is foundational in Jewish and Christian theology: it provides the foundations, the shape of all that follows and the pattern of things and how we should live. And the cornerstone of this pattern is the Sabbath. It is the deliberate "meantime". And it is set apart (made holy). That means it is non-negotiable. Here is not the place to reflect theologically on the rich theme of Sabbath and how it connects with the rest of theology. But if we neglect it, we have begun to undermine, even to kill, the very heart of God's creation. It will not be many steps before we question, challenge and disobey the other "Words of God" (we call them commandments). We will inevitably argue that the end, as we define it, justifies the means. And once this happens in time all hell will be let loose.

Sabbath is a bulwark against the myth that human energy expended in focused ways is ultimately significant, or will achieve the Kingdom of God. We are created among other things to pause, to rest, to reflect. And that makes space for our Creator to re-create us as part of the whole process of universal recreation and rebirth.

To pause in order to consider our place in the scheme of things: our origins, the purpose of our existence: is to connect with the very heart of what it is to be human. Other species are busy in building, saving, mating, giving birth and forming colonies. Only the human species can pause and by the imagination glimpse shafts of understanding about our Source, our true purpose, our origins (Genesis). And this is essential to re-creation.

Far from being a fringe, negotiable, disposable relic of religious tradition, the Sabbath offers a key to comprehending what life is really about. And it is the day of the week, the divine ordinance that resonates most with what we are exploring as the meantime. It may be taking things too far to say that it hallows the meantime; but it is a stubborn and regular reminder that our meantime is close to the heart of God, and to the way his Creation and the Kingdom of Heaven are and function.

All this might remind us that "play" is an activity without direct functional value: it is not undertaken in order to achieve something. And this may help us to see that wholesale re-creation of the world is not from a human point of view something we can do much about. It is God who is doing the re-creation. It might just be the case that we are more pliant and cooperative in his hands when we are playing than when we are busy building our own houses, towers and cities!

PRAYERS

"Lord,
I guess I am a child of my time in finding life leaves little space for what might be called proper Sabbath rest and re-creation. How far, I wonder do what we call worship, or Sunday services, model themselves on your holy Sabbath rest, and facilitate the creative and healthy looking back to our origins?"

"Child,
It is a constant, oft-repeated refrain by those who seek to serve me, and who call themselves by my name, that they so often

struggle in the gap between the Sabbath described in Genesis, and the pressures and assumptions of their contemporary worlds and lives. So often they tend to mirror the ways of human achievements at the expense of its roots in rest and re-creation."

8. Sacrificing

The sacrifices of God are a broken spirit;
a broken and contrite heart,
O God, you will not despise.
PSALM 51:17

Therefore, I urge you, brothers, in view of God's mercy,
to offer your bodies as living sacrifices,
holy and pleasing to God – this is your spiritual act of worship.
ROMANS 12:1

PART OF THE SHARED context of both of these passages of Scripture can be found in the first seven chapters of Leviticus. These are about sacrifices (or "offerings"). All through the Old Testament the importance of sacrifice is repeatedly made clear. The temples were designed with sacrifices in mind, and stone altars for sacrifices were erected before the temples were built. The main purpose of certain sacrifices was to look back to a sin, personal or corporate, intentional or unintentional, to admit it, confess it and to deal with the sin symbolically. The sacrificed animal took the place of the sinner, and the death of the animal represented the penalty of the sin. There were also sacrifices of thanksgiving which recognised God's provision and goodness.

Though sacrifices look forward, in the sense of anticipating a new relationship with God, and a cleansing for service to God, they have their roots in looking back. They are acknowledging that the past has to be dealt with if it is not to warp and inhibit the present and the future.

As the Scriptures unfold, the literal animal sacrifices die out. The Old Testament prophets specifically rail against them: Isaiah spells this out right at the outset of his message: "I have more than enough of burnt offerings, of rams, and the fat of fattened animals; I have no pleasure in the blood of bulls and lambs and goats" (Isaiah 1:11). What God requires is inward repentance, personal sacrifice, not external acts as ends in themselves. In the New Testament the death of Jesus is the one perfect sacrifice of the Lamb of God for the sins of the world – no other sacrifice is necessary to expiate, atone for, or cover, sin.

Much of life in the meantime is about making personal sacrifices in response to the love of God or others. The phrase from Romans comes at the end of the greatest biblical exposition of the love of God in Christ – after pages of majestic description and explanation of God's love and mercy, Paul urges his readers to respond with living sacrifices. I see Romans as the Himalayas of theology – unparalleled in scope and grandeur. "In view of all this ..." is therefore a beautiful way of linking such an image to Paul's injunction. It is the fulcrum of his argument. The term "living sacrifice" is a deliberately dramatic one and would have stopped his original readers in their tracks. Either living or a sacrifice, but not both! That is precisely his point: Christians are to offer their whole lives as a sacrifice.

Paul goes further: this is your reasonable/spiritual service. Literally what he means is that this is what human beings are made for. As the nightingale is designed to sing, or the gazelle is designed to run, as the whale is designed to swim, so is the human being designed to live life as a sacrifice to God. Perhaps the most poignant summary of what it means to be a Christian would be to say that it is a life sacrificed to Jesus Christ in response to his atoning sacrifice for us. C.T. Studd in that often-quoted remark put it like this: "If Jesus Christ be God and died for me, then no sacrifice can be too great for me to make for him."

Sacrifice is a very powerful act and symbol; yet it is part and parcel of everyday life experience. It is an aspect of the fabric of things. Because of love, a committed relationship, loyalty, people will make sacrifices for others. These sacrifices usually prepare the way for another's future, but they do not start in the present – they go back to a committed relationship. "Greater love has no one than this: that he lay down his life for his friend." A mother will, in the normal course of life, make many sacrifices for her children: of time, of effort and in some cases, of food. A politician may resign in order to sacrifice his personal reputation for those of their colleagues. After the invasion by the Argentinians of the Falkland Islands, Lord Carrington, Foreign Secretary of the U.K., immediately resigned so that the price had been paid for allowing this to happen on his watch and the government was able to carry on. A teacher may make sacrifices for her pupils; a soldier may be called upon to make sacrifices for his native land.

In its most concentrated form sacrifice is the willingness to die to oneself in order that another might be freed or empowered. At the end of Charles Dickens novel *A Tale of Two Cities* the hero Sydney Carlton gives his life at the guillotine for the life of his friend. It is an expiation which tells of the sacrifice of the French nation too. And this is a reminder of the way the principle of sacrifice operates at national as well as the personal level. There are times when a generation must sacrifice its well-being for the benefit of others: "For your tomorrow, we gave our today".

One of the most common features of family dynamics where there is trauma and suffering is that one of the family takes the pain and anger, hurt, on him or herself. The rest join in and scapegoat that person. They seem to everyone to be the cause of all the problems whereas often they are what enables the family to survive at all. It is commonly unconscious and so the sacrifice is a silent one reminiscent of the sacrifice of Jesus, the Lamb of God (Isaiah 53:4-6).

One of the great hymns, the great poem in nearly every English hymnbook, is by Charles Wesley: "O thou who camest from above". I quote it here, not for singing, but for meditation on the nature of sacrifice. It is not about a dramatic moment of self-giving, or grand gestures, but about a life that becomes, as Paul urged, "a living sacrifice". And it draws inspiration from Leviticus 6:13: "The fire must be kept burning on the altar: it must not go out".

> *O Thou who camest from above*
> *the pure, celestial fire to impart,*
> *kindle a flame of sacred love*
> *on the mean altar of my heart.*
>
> *There let it for Thy glory burn,*
> *with inextinguishable blaze;*
> *and, trembling, to its source return*
> *in humble love and fervent praise.*
>
> *Jesus, confirm my heart's desire*
> *to work and speak and think for Thee;*
> *still let me guard the holy fire,*
> *and still stir up Thy gift in me;*
>
> *Ready for all Thy perfect will,*
> *my acts of faith and love repeat,*
> *till death Thine endless mercies seal,*
> *and make the sacrifice complete.*

PRAYERS

"Lord,
I don't think I'd realised before how much of ordinary life consists of sacrifice. Perhaps if I were a woman, or a mother, I would have been painfully aware of this fact. There are many whose sacrifices are hidden, unknown and therefore unrecognised and go without thanks or praise. Forgive me for those times and ways in which I miss my true vocation as a human being and help me to steer clear of grand gestures and public sacrifices."

"Child,

Every day, every organisation, every situation and every relationship will provide opportunities for sacrifice. If you haven't noticed this, then you are depending on others to make all the sacrifices for you. It may help you begin to understand this if you look at the sacrifices of Jesus during his life, as well as in his death."

Part 2 DOING

NOW WE TURN our gaze towards the tasks, roles and responsibilities of everyday living in the present. We do not leave the past behind, for much, if not most, daily living has its roots in the past and what has gone before. No individual or group ever starts completely afresh (those that think they do are likely to re-invent the wheel unconsciously again and again!). In this sense time past is nearly always gathered up by the present.

True to the focus and intentions of the whole book, our focus in these eight meditations is not on special activities or accomplishments. We are not singling out famous events or people but continue our exploration of the ordinary, the everyday, the quiet, often unnoticed activities, roles and tasks. A glance through the headings makes this clear. Perhaps we have been so attracted by the "unusual" or "extra-ordinary" (both words are significant here) that we have undervalued the stuff of everyday by default. Many of the parables and much of the teaching of Jesus and the prophets are about everyday activity! But it is so often the miracles and the dramatic stories that grip us.

Perhaps we have seen the "spiritual", the sacred, as distinct from (if not opposed to) the natural or the secular. A besetting sin of every religious leader is to make the life of the fellowship or groups – its meetings, worship, mission, strategies and activities – the centre of attention. If so, the everyday lives and responsibilities of its members are seen as peripheral or marginal. This section reflects the double-edged nature of the final words of the Latin Mass: *"Ite, Missa est!"* It could mean "Go, the service is over". Perhaps that is how it seems to the priest. Or it could mean, "Go, the real service is beginning". That would be a way of seeing it from the point of view of the worshippers. The latter meaning recognises that the living sacrifice of our everyday acts and roles is the real heart of faith and life. Religious gatherings are primarily symbols of God's presence, of our solidarity in him, and of lives surrendered to his will.

While sharing this line of thinking with a group of students in Asia one of them, from Chennai, offered another version of the sending out: "Go: the service is over, and the true worship is beginning"! It nicely inverts the more common meanings or usages of "service" and "worship".

Another duality that we must be aware of is that of contrasting the active and the contemplative. Martha is often portrayed as the embodiment of the active, and her sister Mary the contemplative. In this scheme of things doing is contrasted with being. It was Michel Quoist who was among those who helped me in the lifelong process of seeking to integrate the two. His book, *Prayers of Life*, has been a constant source of insights: "If only we knew how to look at ordinary things all life would become a prayer". How much or little I have learned will become apparent as you read on.

If the distinction between Martha and Mary means a lot to you, and you are drawn to Mary, then you might like to read the section on Being before this one. That makes good sense. As you will see from the introduction to the book it was the intention that Being should be at the centre of the book: its axis or still point. But in a higher scheme of things, Being might well come before Doing. Why don't you browse through both sections and choose for yourself?

1. Parenting

Listen, my son, to your father's instruction
    and do not forsake your mother's teaching.
PROVERBS 1:8

To Timothy, my dear son:

Grace, mercy and peace from God the Father and Christ Jesus our Lord.

I thank God, whom I serve, as my forefathers did, with a clear conscience, as night and day I constantly remember you in my prayers. Recalling your tears, I long to see you, so that I may be filled with joy.
2 TIMOTHY 1:2-4

Then Jesus entered a house, and again a crowd gathered, so that he and his disciples were not even able to eat. When his family heard about this, they went to take charge of him, for they said, "He is out of his mind."
MARK 3:20-21,31-35

MARY'S RELATIONSHIP with her son Jesus forms the basis of this meditation, but before focusing on this unique bond let's pause to acknowledge the universality of parenting. The proverb is not addressed to a literal or biological son but to a pupil and is a reminder of the inextricable link between education and parenting. Paul, likewise, is not Timothy's natural parent but a spiritual father.

We all experience parenting by relatives or other carers, but many people do not become physical parents. If we accept that parenting extends far beyond the particular bond between parent and child there is a sense in which all of us are involved in some parenting at some stage during our lives. I have explored this in the book *The Growth of Love*. A main theme all through and the focus of the final chapter is the maxim that it takes a village to parent. Apart from the extended family roles of uncles and aunts there are the roles of godparent, baby-sitter, teacher and older friend. Perhaps much of the stress in parent-child relationships in western societies comes from seeing parenting as something separate from education, communal living and friendship: this isolates parents and families.

A separation of parenting from civic life will also impoverish the wide network of social relationships interweaving families and family structures. In the best organisations and groups – schools, business, offices, hospitals or sports clubs, some exercise a quasi-parenting role. They will welcome newcomers and help to train and empower them. Jonathan Sacks has pointed out in many of his writings that the moral dimension to human organisations is best seen as not simply something legal or religious but as about the quality of trust, care and mutuality. These qualities are integral to parenting. Almost without exception the subjects of biographies see a person other than their biological parent as a father or mother figure, especially teachers.

Poor parenting and poor attachment of either the biological or psychological sort tend to result in human tragedies, personal and social. The havoc wreaked in the twentieth century by Hitler, Stalin and Mao Tse Tung is a warning to us all. These seriously and dangerously flawed characters came to be seen as substitute parents, their nations as substitute families.

From the twentieth century and large-scale groups let's move back to the tender relationship between Mary and Jesus. In some traditions her role is seen as far more elevated than others. Even so the focus tends to be not so much on her parenting as on her status, virginity and intercessory role. It is rare to stay with her parenting of Jesus much beyond the birth narratives and the Jerusalem episode when as a boy he stayed at the temple after Joseph and Mary had left for Nazareth (Luke 2:41-52).

The passage from Mark's gospel is unique in the gospels and helps to explain the intention of Mary when she wanted to speak with Jesus outside a crowded house. Perhaps we have not imagined what it must have been like for her when the crowd tried to stone Jesus at Nazareth (Luke 4:14-30), or how she felt as the rumour gained ground that he was out of his mind, possessed by Beelzebub. She must have wanted to save him, to shelter him, to bring him back home. Yet somehow she manages to trust him enough to allow him to fulfil the mission in which they both play a part. She follows Jesus to the cross but in no way deflects him from his divinely appointed task.

In the three years of his ministry she has a comparatively minor role for this very reason. Yet this is to undervalue the thirty previous years of his life! As far as we know he spent nearly all that time daily with Mary and family. (There is no indication of any other activity or location between Luke 2:52 (home at Nazareth) and Luke 3:21 (the baptism). So is not his unique ability to listen, to understand women and children, to relate to people intuitively and naturally, something he learned from Mary? Isn't his self-esteem and individuality in some measure due to a good attachment to, and bonding with, her? Some would tend to stress his divinity and the relationship with his heavenly Father here, but why should we attribute everything to this if we have a simple and obvious fact staring us in the face? We know that much of what we are is shaped by human parenting: was it otherwise in the case of Jesus?

The fact that Mary took a back seat in the gospels is an eloquent testimony to the quality of both her character and her parenting. When she does appear it is often because there is an associated crisis or trauma (birth and the killing of the baby boys; Bar-mitzvah and the loss of Jesus; the wedding at Cana and the embarrassment of the wine running out; the attempt to rescue Jesus at Capernaum; the Cross and its unbearable horrors for a loving mother), and this is a reminder of the fact that biological parenting is likely to mean some traumas and anxieties. Perhaps we have overlooked a great truth about parenting in the way we have read the gospels and done our theology: Jesus is who he is, not only because of his divine calling and identity, but because of good parenting, in a close-knit family and village.

Who are those other than our biological mothers and fathers who were like parents to us? And who do we know who see us in a similar role?

PRAYERS

"Lord,
Help me to see and appreciate the quality of Mary's mothering when I read and think about Jesus. Among other things may it be a real antidote to feeling that his activity was everything, rather than an aspect of his nature, being and relationships. And may I never overlook the fortitude of so many single mothers whose lives display such commitment to their children."

"Child,
Remember that of all the ways you may choose to address me, the one that gives me greatest pleasure is that of Abba, Father. When you pray, you will say 'Our Father' won't you?"

2. Working

So Jacob served seven years to get Rachel, but they seemed like only a few days to him because of his love for her.

Jacob lay with Rachel also, and he loved Rachel more than Leah. And he worked for Laban another seven years.
GENESIS 29:20,30

Joseph found favour in his eyes and became his attendant. Potiphar put him in charge of his household and he entrusted to his care everything he owned.
GENESIS 39:4

And Ruth the Moabitess said to Naomi, "Let me go to the fields and pick up the leftover grain behind anyone in whose eyes I find favour."
RUTH 2:2

As Jesus and his disciples were on their way, he came to a village where a woman named Martha opened her home to him. She had a sister called Mary, who sat at the Lord's feet listening to what he said. But Martha was distracted by all the preparations that had to be made. She came to him and asked, "Lord, don't you care that my sister has left me to do the work by myself? Tell her to help me!"
LUKE 10:38-40

THE FOUR EXAMPLES chosen from the Bible represent various aspects of work. Jacob chose to labour long and hard as a shepherd in order to win the hand of his wife in marriage. Joseph had no choice: he was a slave and his responsibilities were urban and organisational. Ruth was effectively a refugee, like a rural street-child dependent on others' left-overs for her survival. Martha (to whom we referred in the previous meditation), is the sister who does the housework, and represents among other things the fact that so much actual work by women is unpaid and goes unrecognised.

Among the many other types of purposeful activity described in the Bible are: preparing ground, sowing, reaping, shepherding and animal rearing, storing and distributing grain, building, finance, housework and hunting, teaching and research (notably Solomon's first "university": 1 Kings 4:29-34), healing and nursing, writing, art, music, sculpture, weaving, judging, fighting, travelling, buying and selling, parenting .... The list is intended to encompass all potential tasks on earth.

Every level of the work hierarchy from slaves and servants, to queens and emperors, including all those in between, is represented. Some are fulfilled and creative in their work (not least Oholiab and Bezalel in building the tabernacle); others are oppressed (e.g. the Hebrew slaves building in Egypt). Given this range and variety it is likely that each of us can find some person, some occupation or some situation with whom or which we can identify. And if we are blighted by the reality or spectre of unemployment there are passages like the parable of the workers in the vineyard, told by Jesus, to confirm that the Saviour has not forgotten those deprived of the opportunity to work. It may be that it is the unemployed who most understand the significance of work: others are often too busy, at the office, factory or with their work friends, to notice.

When "work" first appears in Genesis, it is before the Fall, and is set in the context of the whole of creation. (It is theologically important to note that it was not an unfortunate necessity due to disobedience and sin.) The heavens and stars, the land and waters, the earth and sky, the plants and animals are all specifically mentioned. It is a picture of harmony and balance, an integration achieved by Cezanne perhaps more than any other artist, where the nature and purpose of work is clearly "to co-operate with God in caring for his world". This definition is one that seems so far removed from contemporary realities as to be irrelevant. The focus of work has moved from the steppes, forests and fields into factories, offices, institutions; and now routinely into IT and cyberspace so that for many it has now narrowed to a single chair and computer monitor. Housework is an isolated activity performed alone with a number of gadgets designed to get it done as quickly and efficiently as possible to save time for something else.

No wonder people like Karl Marx were angry about the way in which work demeaned people, put them into conflict with others, and cut them off from the very products of their labour. Sadly his suggested solutions have not proved very practical over time! But collectively and instinctively we know while this is not how things were or are meant to be, in the meantime that is how things are for many of us. So how do we cope with the pressures, the dehumanisation of so much paid work, done usually not as a sense of vocation but in order to get a wage to make ends meet?

This may be where some biblical examples help. Many people were in situations which were not only far from ideal. Some had been captured against their will and were in work for which they were completely unsuited. Jacob was tricked into labouring another seven years for an agreed wage; Joseph was sold into slavery; Ruth was reduced to gleaning because of the death of her husband and ensuing statelessness making her an immigrant: Martha seemed to have housework forced on her by the insensitivity and temperaments of her brother and sister. The overall picture is (as we have come to expect in the Bible) anything but a sentimental or romantic one. How can such unpromising situations be transcended? It has to do with accepting the situation, however long, as God's will for us, and an opportunity (however unlikely) for service to him. The "meantime" may be a lifetime. This is the clear and unequivocal stress of the apostle Paul.

We may resent it; we may see it as unjust; we may work to transform the situation for us and for others. But the fact is that the present reality, the meantime, is one where we can either work for God's glory, or not.

When in Moscow I had the unforgettable privilege of meeting and getting to know Tatiana Velikanova, a close friend of Andrei Sakharov and a professor. After internment in a gulag with Irina Ratushinskaya she was given a new post: teacher in a kindergarten! For a university professor, this new post was meant to be a humiliation. One morning I spent time with her and her colleagues watching and taking photographs. She had put all her considerable knowledge and skill into transforming the kindergarten. She was the best, most sympathetic, radical understanding teacher and colleague I could imagine. It may be beyond most of us in our own strength, but in God's, who knows?

So it is that we recall some of the words of George Herbert, given in full in the Introduction. However quaint they may sound to modern ears, they put this whole attitude to life crisply:

> *Teach me my God and King,*
> *In all things Thee to see;*
> *And what I do in anything,*
> *To do it as for Thee!*
>
> *A servant with this cause*
> *Makes drudgery divine:*
> *Who sweeps a room as for Thy laws,*
> *Makes that and the action fine*

PRAYERS

"Lord,
You know how fulfilled I am in my work but I grieve for others who suffer so much because of unemployment, or unrecognised and unrewarded labours like housework and parenting. Do you not grieve too? Isn't it fundamentally unjust?"

"Child,

This is one of the many, many things that make me grieve deeply as I see the centuries of human history with slave peoples, servants, slaves, and the universal marginalisation of women. Yet there are those, especially women, who have turned even constraints and oppression into expressions of creativity and love. The new world I am shaping will be different from this, so in the meantime, join me as a partner by offering your body as a living sacrifice. In this way you will be following in the footsteps of Jesus."

3. Organising

The next day Moses took his seat to serve as judge for the people, and they stood round him from morning till evening. When his father-in-law saw all that Moses was doing for the people, he said, "What is this you are doing for the people? Why do you alone sit as judge, while all these people stand round you from morning till evening?"
EXODUS 18:13-14

From that day on, half of my men did the work, while the other half were equipped with spears, shields, bows and armour. The officers posted themselves behind all the people of Judah who were building the wall. Those who carried materials did their work with one hand and held a weapon in the other, and each of the builders wore his sword at his side as he worked. But the man who sounded the trumpet stayed with me.
NEHEMIAH 4:16-18

When they landed, they saw a fire of burning coals there with fish on it, and some bread. ... Jesus said to them, "Come and have breakfast".
JOHN 21:9,12

WHEN WE READ these three passages in the context of a meditation on organisation we realise just how easily this element in biblical stories is overlooked. Perhaps we tend to personalise or spiritualise such stories, to stress, say, the wisdom of Moses, or the faith of Nehemiah, the resurrection appearances of Jesus, thus detracting from the way they depict their leadership and organisational abilities.

Organisation and management are contemporary buzz-words. In whatever profession or trade we find ourselves, or would like to be, there is wave upon wave of organisational change: some of it driven by new technology, some by the latest received wisdom on how more output can be achieved more efficiently, some by management gurus. Though settings or tools may differ, the issues of organisation essentially are no different over the centuries. Given a task or series of tasks, given constraints and limitations, what is the best way of organising the human resources?

In the scriptures there is, as we saw in the previous meditation, a wonderful diversity of tasks described: gardening and farming, constructing an ark, building great monuments or cities, framing and maintaining a legal system, making a tabernacle with all its furnishings, arranging journeys, preparing meals and banquets, farming, cleaning houses and so on.

Whether we are executives, managers, labourers, teachers, office-staff, parents, ordinary life has to be organised, and successful organisation demands special skills which some seem to possess and others don't. The abilities of Moses and Nehemiah were exceptional. Here we look at two examples which may help us to re-frame and re-focus our thoughts, and possibly our daily lives. The first is Jesus himself and the second is from the Benedictine Order.

We don't often think of Jesus as an organiser or manager, yet for three years he had the biggest task conceivable: to reconcile the world to God. He had very limited human means, considering he chose to have just twelve disciples, all of whom let him down, an extremely hostile environment (for example Pharisees, Romans or would-be enthusiastic but mistaken followers, and no institution to support the organisation of his ministry). And yet his mission is not only accomplished by the end ("It is finished!"), but each day and each encounter is an expression of the new kingdom and new commandment. Time and again the isolated individual, outcast by others and overlooked, becomes the centre of his attention, as if nothing else mattered. There is no hint of pressure of time or juggling with priorities.

At Passover he had clearly planned what we know as the Last Supper in detail. He asked the disciples to undertake particular tasks as part of his overall plan. And beside Galilee he organised the fishing of his frustrated disciples, prepared a barbecue, got them to bring extra fish, and re-enacted the feeding of the five thousand and the Passover, before engaging in a personal and far-reaching conversation with Peter. It all has the hallmarks of a person who is carefully orchestrating the culmination of his time with those who will continue his work and mission.

To search for a single secret to all this is perhaps to miss the point. But the careful boundary that he organised around the relationship with his Father protected the source of his inspiration, energy, faith and hope. Again and again we find him drawing aside from others in order to be alone with his Father. This is something addressed particularly in Mark's Gospel, for example Mark 3:35 and 14:32-42. It's hard to see how the mission could have been accomplished without it. Setting aside the nature of the spiritual conversations and relationship between them, there was the discipline of time out: a boundary around the world of work, and time set apart (made holy) to reflect upon daily life in tranquillity. It may be that as you ponder this you feel your daily schedule is already bursting at the seams. And yet the challenge of Jesus comes afresh: can you make, say, fifteen minutes each day, and find space to be still in the father's presence? If not, then perhaps you should revise your diary and responsibilities immediately and make space for thirty!

We turn for a second example to the Benedictine Order and other forms of communal religious life. Some years ago I spent a morning among the ruins of Fountains Abbey – one of the most famous of English abbeys. As a member of a residential community the organisation of daily life in such places is always of interest: in all things, from dawn to dusk. What is transparently obvious at Fountains is the attempt to find an integration and balance of every element of life: individual and communal, practical and reflective, celebration and mundane, external and internal. It has to be said, of course, that the abbey is a ruin and there are countless reminders the world over of failed attempts to find and shape that essential balance. Yet isn't something of Benedict's vision of contemporary relevance? In a world of 24/7 activity and communication isn't the way we order our lives increasingly important? "Take from our souls the strain and stress, and let our ordered lives confess the beauty of thy peace" is perhaps even more relevant today than when the words were first written.

It's very easy to get caught in the trap of thinking that organisation is primarily about paid work, person-specifications or job descriptions, and to fail to set the whole of our lives and work in some sort of context shaped by religious faith. It will always stress the overall integration of life and this will lead to practical insights which can be built in to daily life and rhythms.

I am acutely conscious this may sound remote and unhelpful. It is possible that this is a theme where each person needs to work out a practical application for him/herself. If it sounds too fundamental or structural, it is probably because we may need a jolt to some of our assumptions in contemporary society. Jesus always joins us quietly or unostentatiously, as he promised, but as we allow him to share with us, the challenges become more profound.

PRAYERS

"Lord,
I'm honestly not sure if at my life-stage and given the sheer complexity of my life I can build the sort of order and space into daily life I know I ought. Perhaps I can do it at another stage. Isn't this a phase I'll get through?"

"Child,
There is no other place to start than here and no other time

than now. What if Jesus had seen his three years' ministry as a pressured phase when he would jettison his times alone in my presence? Would it be possible to settle on a short daily rendezvous? You name the time and place. I'll be there."

4. Law-abiding

"Hear now, O Israel, the decrees and laws I am about to teach you. Follow them so that you may live and may go in and take possession of the land that the LORD, the God of your fathers, is giving you. Do not add to what I command you and do not subtract from it, but keep the commands of the LORD your God that I give you."

DEUTERONOMY 4:1-2

So on the first day of the seventh month, Ezra the priest brought the Law before the assembly, which was made up of men and women and all who were able to understand. He read it aloud from daybreak till noon as he faced the square before the Water Gate in the presence of the men, women and others who could understand. And all the people listened attentively to the Book of the Law.

NEHEMIAH 8:2-3

Everyone must submit himself to the governing authorities, for there is no authority except that which God has established. The authorities that exist have been established by God. Consequently, he who rebels against the authority is rebelling against what God has instituted, and those who do so will bring judgement on themselves. For rulers hold no terror for those who do right, but for those who do wrong. Do you want to be free from fear of the one in authority? Then do what is right and he will

*commend you. For he is God's servant to do you good. But if you do
wrong, be afraid, for he does not bear the sword for nothing. He is God's
servant, an agent of wrath to bring punishment on the wrongdoer.
Therefore, it is necessary to submit to the authorities, not only because of
possible punishment but also because of conscience.*

*"This is also why you pay taxes, for the authorities are God's servants,
who give their full time to governing. Give everyone what you owe him.
If you owe taxes, pay taxes; if revenue, then revenue; if respect, then
respect; if honour, then honour.*

ROMANS 13:1-7

THE JEWISH FAITH has the Law of God at its heart, and that is one of its greatest gifts to the world. The passage from Deuteronomy is a summary of a vast system of interlocking decrees and laws which was eventually read by Ezra to the whole community in Jerusalem. This reading, one of the turning points of Jewish history, involved repentance and reformation. Near the end of his greatest letter and in the light of his understanding of the relationship of this Law to God's revelation in Jesus Christ, Paul writes about how Christians should live as citizens in a society organised according to Roman law.

Jesus, who understood deeply the Law given in the Jewish Scriptures, interpreted it in a way that stressed motives and attitudes rather than externals. Paul saw the role of "the Law" not as a means of salvation, but more of a schoolteacher leading us to our Saviour. Christians in daily life, however, need to be obedient to the specific laws and authorities in the communities, organisations and nations of which they are a part. The teaching of Paul in his letter to the Romans sets the civil responsibility of Christians within a historical and theological setting. It all sounds so mundane and practical after the grandeur of the rest of his letter! He points out that laws are necessary for civil societies in the world God has shaped.

When you next stop to think about it at a set of traffic lights or pedestrian crossing, you might care to reflect just how much of ordinary life is controlled by laws. There are national and local laws, organisational and institutional rules and the many unspoken traditions and customs of family, friends and neighbours. Usually one can see the benefit of a rule but sometimes it seems irksome or unduly petty or harsh. Before we get uptight about red tape or bureaucracy perhaps we should spare a thought for all those worldwide who would give anything to know just something of the rule of law.

At a given point in time across the world there are millions living in situations where war, famine, oppressive regimes and cultures, have completely disrupted any form of normal social life, equal numbers where organised gangs enforce their own "protection rackets", and many more who live in nations where laws are manifestly unjust toward vast numbers of people. If the biggest complaints we have are about parking restrictions, or tax thresholds, then we would do well to give thanks to God that he has spared us the ravages of lawless societies.

Paul lived under Roman law. It provided him with protection and rights, as well as restrictions, and he may even have died under its sentence. His exhortation to Christians to be obedient citizens is not therefore the idealism of a scholar in an ivory tower, but the practical advice of a much-travelled and wise citizen. It is set in the context of Christ's radical teaching in the Sermon on the Mount (see Romans 12:9-21) and fully committed Christian living under the new covenant of love. But it is also set in the light of newness and importance of the end of the present age (13:11-14).

It is not intended to be a revolutionary manifesto for times of upheaval and change; it is not addressing the exceptional or those living in intolerable and unjust situations. It is for normal life. Put together with the teaching of scripture and the commandments God has given for conducting human life in his world, what challenges do we find in his teaching?

The first is that social life, meaningful and helpful human interaction at every level and kind, needs some form of law/rule/norms. In a far-sighted contemporary essay Peter Berger, a Christian sociologist, tried to imagine a marriage without existing and accepted norms to guide any aspect of conduct. It might sound attractive but it won't work, not least because if everyone tried it there would be no social setting in which the marriage would exist! We need therefore to be tolerant of laws recognising that, though they may be imperfect, they are likely to be more beneficial than the absence of law.

Then there is also the challenge to us all to seek to ensure that the rules we ourselves make (in families, churches, organisations, by voting or representation, in government) are aligned as far as possible with God's law and norms. In a fallen world we can expect rules to favour some against others, to reflect self-interest and a lack of awareness of those on the margins. So here is our responsibility. At election time in democracies the parties all appeal to our own self-interest. It takes an act of will to think of others: the poor of our cities, the elderly, children, and the majority of the human race in the "developing" world.

But the greatest challenge is probably that of living by a higher law than most normal legislation. It is not enough merely to obey the law to not kill, to not steal, to not commit adultery. In everyday life we are challenged to go further than anyone could reasonably expect of us. We are citizens of a holy city. If we give two coats where one is required, or go two miles where one is expected, why worry? In an eternal time-scale it is not significant. So our obedience to specific laws comes from recognising that they are not the sum total of our horizon.

Of course there will be times when we must fight for justice with our lives if necessary, but this is to step out of the meantime into those moments of crisis, upheaval and history. And that is not the purpose of our reflections here.

PRAYERS

"Lord,
I'm just a bit worried that all this may add up to an acceptance of the status quo. Shouldn't I be striving for your kingdom in

everyday life, rather than accepting contemporary anomalies and injustice?"

"Child,
At times that may be so, but more often it is for you to be a responsible citizen. The kingdom is advanced in daily life more than anyone seems to realise. It is not all about tangible progress, revivals and revolutions. Why not use anomalies as a chance to smile? I hope you never gained the impression from Jesus that life and law were to be taken so seriously that a sense of humour was redundant!

5. Giving (and receiving)

Then the whole Israelite community withdrew from Moses' presence, and everyone who was willing and whose heart moved him came and brought an offering to the LORD for the work on the Tent of Meeting, for all its service, and for the sacred garments. All who were willing, men and women alike, came and brought gold jewellery of all kinds: brooches, ear-rings, rings and ornaments. They all presented their gold as a wave offering to the LORD. Everyone who had blue, purple or scarlet yarn or fine linen, or goat hair, ram skins dyed red or hides of sea cows brought them. Those presenting an offering of silver or bronze brought it as an offering to the LORD, and everyone who had acacia wood for any part of the work brought it. Every skilled woman spun with her hands and brought what she had spun – blue, purple or scarlet yarn or fine linen. And all the women who were willing and had the skill spun the goat hair. The leaders brought onyx stones and other gems to be mounted on the ephod and breastpiece. They also brought spices and olive oil for the light and for the anointing oil and for the fragrant incense. All the Israelite men and women who were willing brought to the LORD freewill offerings for all the work the LORD through Moses had commanded them to do.

EXODUS 35:20-29

"Now about the collection for God's people. Do what I told the Galatian churches to do. On the first day of every week, each one of you should set aside a sum of money in keeping with his income, saving it up, so that when I come no collections will have to be made. Then, when I arrive, I will give letters of introduction to the men you approve and send them with your gift to Jerusalem. If it seems advisable for me to go also, they will accompany me."

I CORINTHIANS 16:1-4

THE PASSAGE FROM Exodus communicates a sense of communal joy. And it contains an underlying reminder of the special place of art and beauty in the worship of God. This is, we remind ourselves, a tent that's being made – a provisional structure for the meantime, not a cathedral or temple to last for ever! A rich variety of gifts, talents and materials of both men and women are in evidence, and such a desire to give that Moses eventually had to call a halt to the whole process. What a lovely problem to have! No doubt Paul would have enjoyed having a similar problem in the churches at Corinth and in Galatia. Just imagine him writing: "Please don't give any more. We're having trouble as it is shipping and storing all your gifts to Jerusalem"!

It is probably rare for a human being to give out of pure motives. ("There's no such thing as a free lunch!") There is usually a motive, hidden or unconscious, that can be revealed, and the likelihood that something will be gained in return. A parent gives love and training to a child that can do much for the parent's self-esteem. A benefactor gives to someone or some worthy cause and receives a very grateful vote of thanks. Perhaps reluctantly we see the point: as humans, we are bound inescapably into a network or system, where every act tends to be reciprocal. Pure gift-love is, as C.S. Lewis pointed out in *The Four Loves*, God's prerogative, not ours.

All the same we spend much of ordinary life (out of whatever motive and for whatever reason) giving. This is true in any setting, family, work or leisure. It is also equally true of both secular work, and church life. One of our daughters used to tell us that the offering was the most significant part of a service, and the attention given by churches and Christian organisations worldwide suggests she may have been right! There is more than we might imagine in Paul's letters and the story of the early churches about giving.

Financial giving is only one aspect of the process, however, and in this meditation we focus on the ways in which people give of time and resources to enable life as we know it to function. Forgetting payment and motives so that we can think about giving throws light on life itself. Look back over the past week or two and ask how many people have given of *time*. (How often this is so lavish that it seems wasteful: for example, like the shepherd going after the single lost sheep!) There is the person we stopped to ask the way and who then left no stone unturned to ensure we were on the right path. Or the counsellor or friend who had time to listen until we knew they began to understand. How many people also give of *energy*? The car wouldn't start and there were those who gave it a push to get it going again. Or, another sort of energy, those who used starter leads to turn the engine over. How many people also gave of their *resources*, by way of possessions or information? There is a vast "informal economy" made up of little acts of giving and, by definition, receiving. The most archetypal giving of this sort is probably that of a mother breast-feeding her child.

The list, potentially endless, depends largely on how you categorise giving. And in every action, there is some *self*-giving by definition. We can see it clearly in the carer prepared to sacrifice a job or career in order to help a friend or relative. There is the extra effort of a team member when one of her colleagues is ill or weak. It is less obvious when we think of the assembly line or the office job, the driver on the underground, the official at the job centre. So of what does it consist? The lowest common denominator is that of time, a part of a person's life-span. It won't come back and can't in any exact sense be replaced. Another dimension of this is that with any act or present we empty a little bit of ourselves in the process. It's so obvious in counselling or parenting roles; less so with routine work of serving in a shop or bank. But in each interaction, however small, we have left our own thumb-print on others or the world around us. Great artists and creators do so in a very tangible way. We see their creations and know it is part of them. Many first novels are unconscious autobiographies for example.

Modern societies have become increasingly aware and driven by the market value of everything, including labour. This affects the way we tend to see people, homes, and the language we use, for example the "housing market". That is one of the effects of the "free market" or capitalist system. Commodification, to use a technical term, can obscure the fact that people are still giving of part of themselves in any number of ways without any thought of price. At the extremes we have the British blood donor immortalised by Richard Titmuss in his classic *The Gift Relationship*, or the bomb-disposal expert. We are grateful for the exceptional acts of generosity and self-giving, but overlook the extent of daily ordinary self-giving that might be said to make the world go round.

If we were to write our own autobiographies we would be able to identify times we have given of ourselves without others noticing. It requires imagination and empathy to sense and appreciate the giving of others. The story of the Good Samaritan is a response to a question about giving: who are we obliged to help? So gently and cleverly, that many don't notice, Jesus turned it round and answered it in terms of how we feel as recipients!

PRAYERS

"Lord,

I suppose we do underestimate the degree to which social life is possible only because people are prepared to give. We so easily forget that reward doesn't change the fact that someone has given in the first place. Unemployment must be so destructive if one cannot give anything that is recognised as worthwhile by someone else. Thank you, Lord, for the opportunities my life, yes, even mine, provides the giving. And thank you for all you have given of yourself: more than I can ever repay."

"Child,

Think of the created world and all in it as a gift. Many minds have pondered my motives and have sometimes overlooked the fact that it is given. And this in turn obscures the degree of self-giving or even self-emptying that creation represents. As you remember that it's more blessed to give than to receive, do not forget what difference a gracious recipient makes!"

6. Serving

Now bands from Aram had gone out and taken captive a young girl from Israel, and she served Naaman's wife.
2 KINGS 5:3

"You know that the rulers of the Gentiles lord it over them, and their high officials exercise authority over them. Not so with you. Instead, whoever wants to become great among you must be your servant, and whoever wants to be first must be your slave – just as the Son of Man did not come to be served, but to serve, and to give his life as a ransom for many"
MATTHEW 20:25-28

THE UNNAMED LITTLE serving girl is best known for introducing her master, Naaman the army commander, to Elisha and so to a complete cure of his leprosy. It's such a dramatic story we can easily overlook the measure of her serving. She was a captive, living and working far from her native land. We can only imagine the extent of her daily tasks starting from before dawn to long after dark, and her anguish at being separated from family and community. Yet she was prepared to take the initiative in seeking healing for her master.

The historical setting of this story is surprisingly similar to the social context in which Jesus lived and taught. As a Jew, he was acutely aware of the power and authority of the Roman occupation. To be a servant or a slave at that time was no abstract idea. Later the apostle Paul was to speak of being a slave of Christ: every reader of his original letters would know what that meant in practice, directly or indirectly.

Two thousand years later, and long after the formal abolition of slavery, still a significant proportion of the world's population finds itself in one form of servitude or another. There are domestic servants, children in unsuitable work, vast "factories"/prisons in China, millions of refugees fleeing from oppressors. The list could refer to a whole range of specific cultural contexts the world over.

And once we have acknowledged its worst and most destructive forms we can turn to the way in which some type of serving or servant-hood is part of ordinary everyday life. Most of us find ourselves sometimes serving and sometimes served.

There are very few who are always served by others ... and these are usually megalomaniacs. Even those in senior work positions find it necessary at times to serve others, as well as being servants in other roles in life. Much parenthood is about serving the needs of children, organising one's life as far as possible around them. Over the centuries the role of women has been subservient to that of men, and whatever the cosmetic differences over time the reality is that women still do much of the hidden labour in modern society (collecting water, cleaning, cooking, birthday links and remembering, caring for dependant relatives ...).

The received wisdom is that serving is a second-class and undesirable process or role. One seeks to get out of it if possible. Success is about commanding and directing others, not serving them. This is true of every group, from family to nation-state. Power and authority are essentially the opposite of serving. There have been philosophies, especially Nietzsche's, that have despised servanthood or anything less than the will to dominate others. Feminist movements have been seeking among other things to free women from serving children, or men, or society, simply because they are women. Rights movements are also about freedom, and whatever else they mean they do not include the right to serve!

Into all this, and more, the life and teaching of Jesus comes as a bombshell. It needs very careful interpretation and understanding if we are to apply it aright. But there is no doubt that the Messiah was seen as the one who would free Israel from slavery; a leader who would lead and triumph over his enemies. He would have something of the power of David and the grandeur of Solomon. Jesus digs beneath the surface and sees in the Suffering Servant of later Isaiah the true nature of Messiahship. As the Son of Man he is to be a leader, but he turns the whole concept of leadership on its head. He is to serve; to wash his disciples' feet; to cook them a meal; and eventually to die for them, for women, children, Gentiles and slaves. Perhaps our familiarity with the texts denies us the sense of surprise and shock we should feel at the breathtaking contrast between the concepts of lordship and servant-hood.

A family friend of mine was a member of the Hitler Youth Movement and he kept the pledge he signed on joining. He swore total allegiance to Hitler as his lord and father and promised to lay down his life, if necessary, for the Fuhrer. The contrast with the leadership of Jesus could not be more complete. He takes upon himself the humble role of shepherd, willing to lay down his life for the sheep! My friend did not have to die, although it was a close-run thing; Jesus, as we know, did die, as the climax of his servant Messiahship.

Often focusing on the drama and uniqueness of Calvary can obscure the fact that serving (in denying oneself in order to care for and help others) was such a fundamental part of the daily life of Jesus. Quite apart from positions where it is an enforced role, the act of serving is necessary for the survival of social and communal life. Jesus challenged us to take up the cross daily. It is largely unnoticed (by others generally and certainly by media headlines and stories) and usually unrewarded in any obvious sense. But if accepted and embraced it proves the basis for true healing, sharing, growth and greatness. The setting of a small residential community provides all the insights needed into this truth. The processes are the same in any group.

For the community to function there have to be those who will put the needs of others quietly and consistently before their own. Any number of practical jobs can be done – if done well, not noticed – and a night's rest or plans for a personal pleasure sacrificed because of the demands of a situation. If people insist on doing only their fair share of work then community is impossible: that is the nature of human interdependence. There is something equivalent to friction (in Newtonian physics) that operates in the social world: fairness and equality are never enough. Those with greatest responsibility will also have to serve most, however little that serving is noticed. This brings us back to the Suffering Servant:

> *"He had no beauty or majesty to attract us to him ...*
> *He was despised, and we esteemed him not."*
> ISAIAH 53:2-3

Paul was without doubt one of the greatest leaders and shapers of the Christian faith, yet the title he most cherished was that of servant or slave of Christ. And what drew him was not the glory of false Messiahship, but the grace of Jesus that led him to lay down his life for others: "while we were still sinners, Christ died for us." (Romans 5:8). Like Paul, as we seek to serve others in any number of practical ways, we are living out the principle of life and growth: "Unless a seed falls into the ground and dies it abides alone; if it dies it brings forth much fruit."

PRAYERS

"Lord,
I can accept this for myself (if not enthusiastically!) for I take the general point. But all the time I am appalled by the sheer injustice and all forms of oppression: the insensitivity of organisations and institutions that force some (the majority) to serve others. The two-thirds world is in effect serving the so-called developed world at this very moment with its cheap labour, commodities and debt repayment. Does this sort of serving become justified in the light of this concept of servant-hood, I wonder"

"Child,
You have begun that long and difficult process of seeking to stand in the place of others. The enforced slavery or servanthood of anyone on the grounds of their gender or race or status or creed you know offends and grieves me deeply. But the principle goes through every stratum and caste. As people strive for justice, may they recognise that justice and equality are not enough. By the way, should you ever join in the struggle at the deep end, don't be surprised if you find me there even though you didn't read about it in your headlines!"

7. Forgiving

When Joseph's brothers saw that their father was dead, they said, "What if Joseph holds a grudge against us and pays us back for all the wrongs we did to him?" So they sent word to Joseph, saying, "Your father left these instructions before he died: 'This is what you are to say to Joseph: I ask you to forgive your brothers the sins and the wrongs they committed in treating you so badly.' Now please forgive the sins of the servants of the God of your father." When their message came to him, Joseph wept.
GENESIS 50:15-17

"This, then, is how you should pray:

'Our Father in heaven,
hallowed be your name,
your kingdom come,
your will be done
on earth as it is in heaven.
Give us today our daily bread.
Forgive us our debts,
as we have also forgiven our debtors.
And lead us not into temptation,
but deliver us from the evil one.'

*For if you forgive men when they sin against you, your heavenly Father
will also forgive you. But if you do not forgive men their sins, your
Father will not forgive your sins."*

MATTHEW 6:9-15

J OSEPH HAD SUFFERED chronically and terribly as a result of his brothers'
jealousy and scheming. He had been sold into slavery in a foreign land,
and ended up in prison. His precious relationship with his father had
been broken when they feigned Joseph's death. Over time his brothers
come to be in no doubt about the enormity of what they have done, and
when Jacob dies they fear the worst – what if Joseph has been waiting for
this moment when he can seek just revenge? Joseph weeps because he has
already forgiven them (Genesis 45) and now he realises that their duplicity
and fear have prevented them understanding and accepting his forgiveness. It may be they have never forgiven themselves for what they did.

There are other times in the Scriptures when forgiveness is requested,
offered, received and accepted. One of the most well known is when Moses
offers his own life if only God will forgive the people of Israel. A lesser-
known example is the prayer of Solomon at the dedication of the temple.
He prays for personal forgiveness and for the forgiveness of the nation of
Israel and every individual who seeks for mercy in it (1 Kings 8:22-40). And
we all know of the centrality of forgiveness in God's relationship with his
creation especially as it is revealed in the life and death of Jesus. The Lord's
Prayer enshrines forgiveness in both our relationship with God and with
others. They are two sides of the same coin, however much we might wish
they could be separated!

As you read this you may be hurting deeply, and be very angry. There is
so much hurt and injury around that it is very possible you know you
should be forgiving someone and simply cannot find it in your heart. You
are too upset. It has cost too many tears and too much pain. Perhaps it is
the other party in a relationship, one of your family, or a colleague at work.
You understand all too well why many Jews cannot and will not pray for
the forgiveness of the Nazis who sought to exterminate their race, or those

on both sides in Northern Ireland who have suffered too much violence to forgive "the others".

On the other hand the hurt may be caused by the realisation that someone else has not forgiven you. They continue to bear a grudge against you. You know you did wrong in a hasty moment and the rift has, if anything, grown over time. Hard as it might be to say it, these two kinds of forgiveness are relatively straightforward, if not easy. For they involve conscious actions – you have offended; you have been offended and both parties know it.

The going gets more murky, and the undergrowth deeper, when we come to consider unconscious acts or attitudes. Though someone has been unaware of it, they have always looked down on you, been critical, perhaps from childhood and they don't know how hard you have tried to forgive them, and how much they need forgiveness. The other way round means that there are people you have caused hurt and pain and you simply don't realise it. The chances are it's those who are your nearest and dearest, those you have known for so long.

And this is where the prayer of Jesus is so real and challenging: "Father, forgive them for they know not what they do!" At first sight it might seem to involve just the soldiers and bystanders at the cross, but across the centuries it rings out in every heart and home. He is praying for each person, each family, and each community. As he took on himself the sin, anger, hurt and injustice of the world he accepted all those unconscious acts of unkindness and judgement, or thoughtlessness and anger, and he asks his Father to forgive us and our fellow human beings.

This is crucial to our understanding of what it is to be a human being and a Christian. We need to come daily before our Lord asking for and receiving his forgiveness, because we simply do not know and cannot fathom what we have done. As we receive his forgiveness he helps us to understand what we have done, and this in turn releases us to forgive others and to seek their forgiveness. There's nothing one way about forgiveness. You won't find someone who is always forgiving others without asking for forgiveness. The awareness of the need to forgive and receive forgiveness is at core self-awareness.

Social groups have similar dynamics to individuals. No club or association can function without forgiveness built into institutional structures and processes. There comes a time when "an eye for an eye and a tooth for a tooth" has to be replaced by forgiveness if wounds are to be healed and progress is to be made. No break in foreign relations is ever restored without a measure of forgiveness. This is about a certain give and elasticity in structures that enables wrongdoing to be absorbed. It happens in families. The offender has to have the chance of rehabilitation, and a group or nation must be given the opportunity to begin anew. Justice is necessary but it is not enough. Thank God that, in this world and his dealings with us, justice is ultimately set in the context of his atoning grace and forgiveness.

PRAYERS

"Lord,
As I pause before you now there is a glimpse of the magnitude of my unconscious sins. If much of my life is in one respect unconscious as far as I am concerned, who knows what I have done by deeds done or left undone. I see the way others cause hurt and distress, but what about me?"

"Child,
In any relationship that involves real sharing you become aware of yourself through the other's forgiveness. When you responded to my love I already knew your deepest unconscious fears and desires. They are all accepted, and forgiven – as far as you will let me. Don't focus on yourself however (I do that) but concentrate on forgiving others. The rest will follow as clear air follows a storm."

8. Laughing

Then the LORD said, "I will surely return to you about this time next year, and Sarah your wife will have a son."

Now Sarah was listening at the entrance to the tent, which was behind him. Abraham and Sarah were already old and well advanced in years, and Sarah was past the age of childbearing. So Sarah laughed to herself as she thought, "After I am worn out and my master is old, will I now have this pleasure?"

Then the LORD said to Abraham, "Why did Sarah laugh and say, 'Will I really have a child, now that I am old?' Is anything too hard for the LORD? I will return to you at the appointed time next year and Sarah will have a son."

Sarah was afraid, so she lied and said, "I did not laugh."

But he said, "Yes, you did laugh."

GENESIS 18:10-15

"... a time to weep and a time to laugh,
    a time to mourn and a time to dance."

ECCLESIASTES 3:4

THERE ARE VERY different types of laughter, some laden with disbelief like that of Sarah, some inspired by another's misfortune, some cynical, some the result of an incident or story that so amuses and delights that it is for all to share, some mixed with tears and deep-seated joy.

Many have assumed that religion is a serious business and that the Bible is a doom-laden, pious ("bible-black", to quote Dylan Thomas) book, about a wrathful God condemning a fallen world. This includes both critics and believers. The exercise of studying every verse of the Bible was an eye-opener in this respect for me. As a student of literature I recognised the range of genres represented, but as one who had so often heard the scriptures read or expounded in a church setting I had probably underestimated the amount of humour it contains. I shouldn't have been so surprised, for as a boy I often listened to Dr. Martyn Lloyd-Jones preach at Westminster Chapel and he frequently alluded to "divine humour", as he called it. And while at Oxford, Malcolm Muggeridge reminded us more than once that the editor of *Punch* had an impossible job because real life was so much more absurd, so much more comical than anything invented. Given that the Bible is such a historical book earthed in real life the humorous vein is only to be expected.

In the novel *The Name of the Rose*, by Umberto Eco, there is a discussion about Jesus and whether he ever laughed. An old monk is convinced that because the gospels don't record him doing so, he didn't. His protagonist finds it inconceivable that someone as alive and witty and imaginative as Jesus didn't laugh. And that is how I see him. While living in Edinburgh I saw an early version of the musical *Godspell*. It has since become an accepted part of musical history, but then it was risqué. Why? In large measure because Jesus was portrayed as a clown, always ready to see the funny side of situations. Significantly it always seemed to be the religious leaders who failed to understand the essentially humorous nature of so much human activity.

Ordinary life is made bearable, made enjoyable, because of laughter. Without trying to develop a theory of laughter and jokes, which tends among other things to kill them stone dead, it may be worth beginning by acknowledging what a deep, precious and unifying quality humour is. One of the girls who joined our community as a teenager had difficulty understanding why people laughed. I observed to her that she often laughed even so. She replied that she only did this when she saw others laughing. In fact she had no idea at all why they found anything funny. (She had, significantly, been separated from parents and friends for a substantial time when she was very young and ill in hospital, and had suffered physical abuse.)

During the 1990s a phenomenon emerged in many English churches loosely described as, and deriving from, what was known as the "Toronto blessing". It manifested itself in various ways including seemingly uncontrollable types of behaviour including shaking, falling down, making animal noises and crying ... and laughing. As a sociologist of religion I was intrigued to notice that it was largely a western phenomenon occurring among people who have tended to see religion as a controlled, serious, reverent and organised affair. One of the functions of "the blessing" seemed to be to allow them to link their religious insights and experiences with expressive human behaviour (with the exception of the rather strange and worrying animal noises) into their religious life and worship.

Jewish culture is essentially expressive, full of celebration and repartee. Rabbinical discussion is imbued with much subtle humour (as the BBC broadcasts and writings of Rabbi Lionel Blue testify) and so to understand Scripture we need to be aware of the puns, the caricatures, the allusion and witticisms that enliven many Bible pages. Unless we can read the Scriptures in their original languages much will remain obscured, but despite that, if we are sufficiently aware even some of the most learned and sacred books like Proverbs and Psalms are alive with witticisms and puns. As for Jesus and his stories – they are positively bursting with wit and humour.

One of the readiest indicators of the health and well-being of a person or group is the ability to laugh and see the funny side of things. It's a way of coping with the peculiarities, incongruities, stresses and conflicts of life. If we pause to reflect on the groups of which we are a part: family, church, work, committees, clubs: it may become apparent how common laughter and humour are in the ordinary course of things. It's impossible to function without humour and so someone needs to do something if it's missing. Could you and I do anything to help? Perhaps it sounds like stereotyping but the three cities and cultures where I find the most infectious humour are Dublin, Liverpool and Glasgow - they have a lot in common, not least their cosmopolitan and Roman Catholic components. It couldn't be that Protestantism has tended to undervalue this element of the faith, could it?

Of course some of us are constitutionally more able to see the funny side of things than others. We may be blessed with family and communal histories which enable us to enter unconsciously into the wit and joy of shared (but unspoken) experiences and values. It may be that is not our lot. If so, we can at very least rejoice indirectly as we see others united, whether in poverty or wealth, easy or hard lives, laughing together. That will then encourage us in the belief that there is a funny side of things, even if we can't see it from where we sit.

PRAYERS

"Lord,
When I'm tense and stressed the humour goes out of life. I suppose Martha with her devoted, earnest but humourless service of the Master typifies my experience at such times. How on earth do I or you or someone inject laughter into such times without it sounding hollow?"

"Child,
There is a time to laugh and a time to weep. There is also much time in between. To laugh you have to relax a little bit, to step out of the immediate, the present, if only for an instant. It's rather like prayer in fact. And, just for your interest, human prayers are rarely witty or fun. For some reason people think it's a serious, devotional, concentrated business all the time. Where do you think that whole idea came from?"

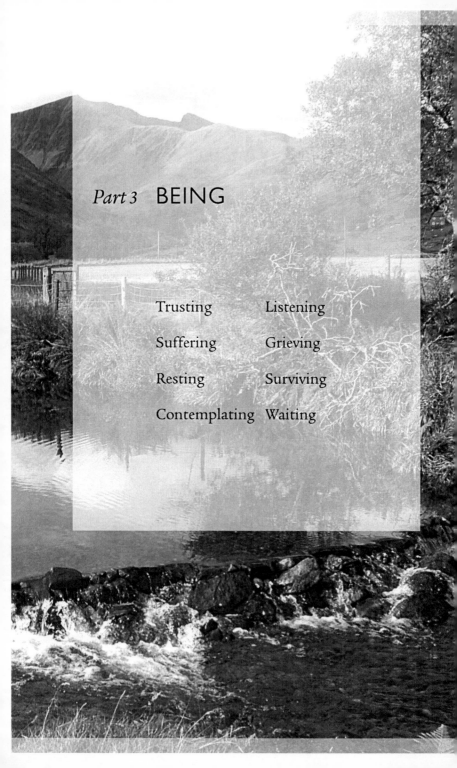

Part 3 BEING

O N REFLECTION "human being" can seem an ironic way of describing *homo sapiens*: "human doing" would be more apt. Contemporary life is characterised by anything but being. Life seems to be all about the activities described in Part 2 and many more. All the same we share an awareness that deep down being is at the heart of what it means to be human. And that, as I explained in the Introduction, is why this section on being is the centre of this book. Humans share with every animal species instincts for reproduction, for security and for survival. One of the things that distinguish us from them is our ability to be still and to be conscious of ourselves, the outside world, and of God. "Be still and know that I am God" (Psalm 46:10) addresses us at the core of our essence and being. Such stillness is not something most of us experience commonly or naturally. It seems to need a crisis or effort, guidance or practice, and it is not easily described. Those who experience it *know*; those who do not experience it do not know. And those who do not understand it are unlikely to value it.

T.S. Eliot was one who both understood and managed to describe it. His *Four Quartets* provided much inspiration for these meditations. In these he talks in that beautifully evocative phrase of "the still point of the turning world". This is his way of describing "now", when there is that poise that allows momentary integration of past and present, of inner and outer worlds, of body and spirit, awareness of self and lack of self-consciousness, of mind and emotion. He knew that this was the desired experience or state of world religions and traditions, and thus appeared to be unattainable to all but the initiated few. But it is closer to ordinary life than most recognise or dare to believe. An illness, an unexpected delay or turn of events and we are taken out of the routine of life and we are faced with ourselves in a new way. It is not just about the absence of work or activity, but about a quality of awareness alive to inner realities and relationships.

When God revealed his name to Moses, he revealed his nature: the image in which men and women are made. He did not reveal himself as the Creator, although he creates; the Redeemer, although he redeems; the Shepherd, although he leads; the Father, although he loves. He revealed himself as "I am that I am": the God of being. Only in discovering the riches of Being is it possible to begin to be aware of that of God in each of us and in his world. And that discovery is more likely to be made in the meantime than in moments of ecstasy, achievement or activity.

1. Trusting

As Pharaoh approached, the Israelites looked up, and there were the Egyptians, marching after them. They were terrified and cried out to the LORD. They said to Moses, "Was it because there were no graves in Egypt that you brought us to the desert to die? What have you done by bringing us out of Egypt?" Moses answered the people, "Do not be afraid. Stand firm and you will see the deliverance the LORD will bring you today. The Egyptians you see today you will never see again. The LORD will fight for you; you need only to be still."

EXODUS 14:10-14

Hezekiah trusted in the LORD, the God of Israel.

2 KINGS 18:5

THE MOMENT OF STILLNESS described in Exodus comes between two great, unparalleled and unforgettable events: the Passover night when the people of Israel left Egypt, and the crossing of the Red Sea. All through the Scriptures, in worship and festivals the Passover and crossing of the Red Sea are celebrated and recalled. The pause between the events is scarcely noticed. Yet in it Moses is as aware of his closeness to God as at any time in his life, with the exception of the burning bush.

The plight of the chosen people is desperate and potentially tragic by any standards. After generations the Israelites have finally been released from slavery in Egypt. God has intervened miraculously. The Exodus has taken place. Or has it? Before they know it the people find themselves confronted by the Red Sea ahead, and a massive and well-equipped avenging army behind. There is no choice; there is no other option. They cannot fight; they cannot swim. They have to stand still and to trust the Lord God Almighty.

Hezekiah was king of Judah at a similarly dramatic and potentially disastrous moment of Jewish history. The northern kingdom had been conquered by Assyria and the vast Assyrian army was poised to invade Judah and take Jerusalem. Isaiah tells him to trust the Lord Almighty. Against all the odds (see 2 Kings 19:35-36) he prophesies that the city of Jerusalem will be saved.

In the meantime there was nothing to do but to be still; to wait; to trust. And that is often how we discover the nature of being: it is not something we choose, so much as something thrust upon us. The catalyst may be a personal trauma, a friend's illness, a broken relationship, a death in the family, the loss of a job. Everything that has been taken for granted is swept from under our feet and there is no escape. It is as though forces of chaos have been unleashed, the waters seem overwhelming, monsters of the deep rise up to threaten. Problems seem to arrive in legions, threatening with their advance.

It is in the midst of fear that the first dawning awareness of "being" can come. And it brings with it dim echoes of our past experiences as children. For as children there is a primal fear that we will be engulfed by chaos and separated from the parent who alone can protect us. Every separation, every trauma threatens our very existence, our being, and it is only trust that stands between us and overwhelming chaos. We need to know that we are "held", that no matter how furious and strong the forces that threaten us, the arms that hold us are stronger. This is the essence of "being": we cannot escape; we cannot act or plan a way out. We must be still, with hands over our eyes and covers over our heads, as it were, and trust our Father.

A little girl I know never experienced that firm safety and trust in her early years. For years she experienced primal fear, especially on our sailing dinghy. No matter who was with her, no matter what assurances were given or the sense of peace and well-being that others felt, she could not trust anyone or the water, however calm. Significantly her life outside the dinghy was characterised by a restless anxiety – an inability to relax, to enjoy the now, to be. Conversely the story is told of another girl who was leaning over the bow-rail of a ship during a very rough voyage. She seemed oblivious to the combined forces of wind and waves as she stood alone. A fellow passenger struggled to her through the spray with the intention of persuading her away from the rail. "It's all right," the girl replied, "My dad's the captain of this ship. That's him on the bridge."

It may be as you read this you find yourself, like Moses, in a situation where you will have to be still, and to trust God. Perhaps you don't feel anything like the captain's daughter, quietly confident at the bow of the liner. If so, there is a special encouragement from the stories of Moses and Hezekiah. Despite their positive qualities, both men were both full of anxiety and doubt. They trusted God because they had no choice. And this may be exactly how it is with you. Paradoxically this is the setting where the process of being can begin. When we cannot run, or hide, or bury ourselves in business, then we find ourselves in the presence of the One whom we know we must trust. And his presence is that of the unchanging, unfailing "I Am". It is not a time for planning or action, but a time of being. There may be tears, but it can also be a time of extreme self-consciousness when there is a heightened awareness of something as basic as breathing. If so it is an experience which can lead to the stillness which is the heart of being, and the knowledge that he is God.

PRAYERS

"Lord,
 If you really want to know the truth, the last person I identify
 with is the captain's daughter. So often I feel only the lash of
 wind-driven rain in my heart, and a heavy swell full of primal

fear. I am not still. I cannot trust ... I want to, of course, but the chaos is threatening to overwhelm me. It might just as well be armies marching against me. I feel that helpless and powerless. Please don't tell me to pray, to meditate. If you do you just don't understand how frightened I really feel."

"Child,
I hear your pounding heartbeat. It tells me everything. It cannot forever race like this. You will be still. You must be still, and I am with you however long it takes. Why don't you pour out everything and trust me with your anger and hurt as it is? You're not going anywhere at present, and neither am I. Let's wait together, let your mind race and your body feel the fear. I will wait for you however long it takes you to be still and know that I am ...."

2. Listening

"Be ever hearing, but never understanding: be ever seeing, but never perceiving. Make the heart of this people calloused; make their ears dull and close their eyes. Otherwise they might see with their eyes, hear with their ears, understand with their hearts, and turn and be healed."
ISAIAH 6:9-10

"Those who have ears, let them hear."
MATTHEW 13:9

THESE WORDS OF JESUS are his most often repeated message. Again and again he ends a story or some teaching with them, and again and again his hearers, like us, tend to miss or overlook what he really means. Isaiah pointed out that people could hear what was being said without understanding the message, and Jesus repeatedly quoted this part of Isaiah.

It was only after about fourteen years of teaching in a theological college that I began to discover what it was that I really wanted to teach! The courses for which I was responsible were about the contemporary context of Christian leadership and ministry, embracing some sociology, psychology and psychiatry. Their purpose was to ensure that the message, methods and work of the students were relevant and alive in the real world; its shops, offices, schools, neighbourhoods and families. Gradually it dawned on me that the single most important factor in ensuring a relevant ministry was the art of listening. If we do not listen any message, method or programme can be out-of-date or irrelevant. I made the course more open-ended, less packed with content, more geared to dynamics and relationships. Those students who voiced their concern, usually by commenting that they wanted to move on, to find answers, to be practical, were the ones who were in most need of developing the ability to listen. They were also the ones least aware of their inability to listen.

And that's part of the problem: the worst listeners are the ones least likely to hear others pleading with them to listen! They are often characterised by their desire to pass on their own thoughts, full of unconscious regrets about the past or anxieties about the future. We need to learn the art of being before we can begin to listen. Our heart has to be still before we can hear the heartbeat of another. We have to make space for another voice, other priorities, other perspectives, if we are to hear another's message. As long as our own agendas, with our own unconscious fears and needs, dominate our minds and hearts, there is simply no way we can tune in to anyone else.

Some of the wisest psychiatrists and therapists had special routines before they had a session with a client. In order to listen fully and fairly to the person coming to see them they acknowledged their need to divest themselves of their own memories and desires. It was said that Carl Rogers used to go to a window, open it and symbolically throw away his own agenda. In ordinary life and daily encounters we need to be equally receptive if we are to hear the real messages of others. It requires acute listening skills to hear the music between the notes, the words between the lines, echoes of memories, whispers of uncertainty.

Listening is a gift, but it can also be learnt to some degree. One very practical way is to repeat or paraphrase what someone else has said in order to check how accurately their message has been received. Like trusting, it may be we find ourselves in situations where we simply have to listen. As a parent we find a child has done something, has said something that stops us in our tracks. What on earth do they mean? We trust the child enough to pause and reflect on the meaning of what they say. Perhaps music is something which can help us to listen: I don't mean popular music with its hypnotic melodies and rhythms, its stereotypic lyrics, but some of the more profoundly challenging music - jazz, blues, rap, romantic, classical. On first hearing some of Beethoven's Late Quartets one wonders what form they have, what possible meaning or unity. As you listen the themes and resonances become clearer. It's all there, but can only be experienced by concentrated, and repeated, listening.

Some years ago I settled myself on some rocks in the middle of a mountain stream near the Rhinog Mountains in Snowdonia. It was a Sunday afternoon and there was plenty of time to be alone. I lay down and started to listen to the noise of the stream. At first it sounded simply like anything you would expect (a rushing stream perhaps?), but slowly I began to hear some of the individual sounds that made up the whole. There was a rhythmic 'plop' near the centre of a pool; a tinkling some way down-stream; a gushing or hissing between two rocks and so on until I detected more than eight distinct sounds. No doubt there were more, but in fifteen minutes, for the first time in my life, I had listened to a stream. I thought I had heard often before. Once I truly began to hear this little stretch of one particular stream I realised my "listening" was little more than a way of confirming my own preconceptions and stereotypes.

It's often those people we meet most and know best whom we find it hardest to hear. And God, who is so close to us, that we usually take him for granted, finds it immensely difficult to get his message through. He tries in every sort of way - using all the resources of creation, his world, his word, his Son, his people, but still we fail to hear. Perhaps we should stop and listen to one story from his word; to focus on one question we want to ask him; to shout in pain or anguish until we hear some sort of response. We may find there's someone or something speaking for him ... if we can listen.

PRAYERS

"Lord,

I'm not such a bad listener. I can think of worse! And yet I'm better at speaking and telling others what I feel and think. You've forced me to be still; I trust you. What else can I do? Will you speak? I really am trying to listen ..."

"Child,

Like that ever-flowing mountain stream, I am speaking to you day by day. I am listening to your heartbeat still. Sometimes there is simply no chance of you hearing me or anyone else. But now you are learning to be, you are learning that it's not words you must listen for. You must listen to the space between them. Don't be afraid of silence. Don't be put off by crowded noises. You want to hear. Be still and listen to the next person or creature you meet, as if it were me ... you never know!"

3. Suffering

"Yet if I speak, my pain is not relieved;
and if I refrain, it does not go away.
Surely, O God, you have worn me out;
you have devastated my entire household. ...
My face is red with weeping,
deep shadows ring my eyes;
yet my hands have been free of violence
and my prayer is pure. ...
My spirit is broken,
my days are cut short, ..."
JOB 16:6-7,16-17; 17:1

"Is it nothing to you, all you who pass by?
Look around and see.
Is any suffering like my suffering
that was inflicted on me,
that the Lord has brought on me
in the day of his fierce anger? ...

"This is why I weep
and my eyes overflow with tears.

No-one is near to comfort me,
 no-one to restore my spirit. ...

People have heard my groaning
 but there is no-one to comfort me."
LAMENTATIONS 1:12,16,21

UCH OF THE BIBLE, much of history, much personal experience, is permeated or contorted by suffering. It is worth pausing to reflect on just how much suffering there is – otherwise we may have a completely skewed view of our own and others' pain and discomfort. The books of Job and Lamentations are in certain respects exceptional because of the degree of suffering they describe and seek to address. In other respects they are focusing on a human experience familiar to all, at every page of history. The story of the Jews is a story of wave after wave of anguish, rejection and pain. The life of Jesus culminates in perhaps the most total and acute pain ever encountered on earth and the New Testament churches knew much from personal experience of wounds and pain.

Not that suffering is everything, but that it is encountered by every human being at some stage, personally or through others. For some, there are years of constant, indescribable, throbbing pain and anguish. For others there is some relief. For still others most of life is free from all but occasional stabs of pain like toothache or an accident. As I write these words I am in the Accident and Emergency Department of a London hospital: I am surrounded by people in all sorts of conditions. Some are experiencing pain themselves; others are crying because of the suffering of others. A mother leans on the shoulder of her husband. He is holding their child's teddy bear while the child is being treated. The whole scene is a microcosm of the world. Meanwhile most people are at home, many watching television, completely unaware of the suffering going on.

Perhaps as you read this it may be that personal suffering is a distant memory. On the other hand the words from Job and Lamentations may speak with raw and uncanny accuracy of your own predicament – personal, or felt, through someone close to you. It can be an experience where it is impossible either to be still or to listen. And yet the only way of coming to terms with suffering is a quality of *being* rather than *doing*. It has to be accepted rather than denied. Extreme suffering cannot be denied. It cuts a person off from others, from the rest of life, but it has to be shared with someone or something.

Always nagging away over time are questions of justice, meaning and causes: why me? Why does God allow such suffering? The book of Job is one of the profoundest explorations of such a theme, and in a remarkable way it addresses such issues without ever denying the pain, the threat of chaos, the loneliness of suffering. The biggest frustration we feel on reading the drama of Job is not so much the pain and losses of Job as the sheer inability of his friends to enter sufficiently into his situation to feel the pain and anguish he is going through.

No "answers" can be given to the person experiencing suffering. The powerful insights of C.S. Lewis in *A Grief Observed* and *The Problem of Pain* show ultimately that to proffer an answer is to be outside the pain, to be an observer, and analyst. From the inside there is no comfort from reasoned arguments or well-meaning advice. So where does that leave us as we writhe in the crucible of pain, as we experience the fiery furnace, the deep waters, of suffering? It leaves us with our pain, with the loneliness of our predicament, but there is a shaft of comfort that shines into our being. We may feel absolutely cut off from others; we may be tortured almost past endurance by pain. But we are not alone. If the incarnation of Jesus Christ has anything to teach it speaks of a God who knows the pain and isolation, not because he has heard our cries or the prayers of others, but because he is on the inside actually feeling our wounds.

If we suffer, he suffers. And in this shared suffering there is a quality of being we cannot experience from the outside. We are welded together by the shared pain. And it works both ways: our suffering can bring us closer to others as well as giving a way of knowing whether they really identify with us. Job's friends cannot identify with him, nor he with them. But the writer of Lamentations finds that the corporate suffering of Jerusalem leads deep into an understanding of God's presence and love. In the depths of loss and pain the great truth is discovered: "Great is thy faithfulness".

Some of the closest human relationships are forged through pain and loss, not through words, or comfort but suffering jointly experienced. In his hours of greatest personal anguish Jesus did not ask his disciples to speak to him or pray for him, but to "Watch with me". He calls us to identify with others in empathy and to recognise those who watch with us.

It has often, perhaps too often, been said that great pressure is one of the major factors in the formation of diamonds. It is certainly true that shared suffering can bring a completely new awareness of self and others.

One of the inevitable effects of suffering is that it strips away all the inessentials of life. What once seemed important is, in the crucible of experience, now shown to be dross. It doesn't lessen the pain, or ameliorate the hurt, but it does concentrate the mind. After the pain life looks different: problems before the pain now seem less insurmountable: what was experienced as severe deprivation is bearable and shared with others; what provoked anxiety is now faced with fortitude or quiet confidence.

Our local hairdresser spent nearly the whole of the Second World War as a prisoner of war in Germany. He saw and experienced extreme hardship. It has left its scars. But it has also affected his basic attitude to life. He never grumbles whatever the situation and he is always aware of the lot and suffering of others. He would never have sought internment, and he hopes, of course, that it will never be repeated, but through it he has found deep insights, hidden strengths and an understanding of others.

PRAYERS

"Lord,
Help me. Lord, help me. I don't ask for pity or for answers. But I do ask that you will give me the strength to face today, some sign that you are with me. And should it happen, please help

me to listen to those who face different trials, lesser or greater than mine."

"Child,
I know your suffering from the inside.
I am with you.
We are closer than ever before.
The weight that prevents you from doing, planning, hoping, is teaching you, whether you like it or not, about being. Accept your suffering. Embrace it. You have nothing to fear. I am with you."

4. Grieving

By the rivers of Babylon we sat and wept
    when we remembered Zion.
There on the poplars we hung our harps,
for there our captors asked us for songs,
    our tormentors demanded songs of joy;
      they said, "Sing us one of the songs of Zion!"
How can we sing the songs of the LORD
    while in a foreign land?
If I forget you, O Jerusalem,
    may my right hand forget its skill.
May my tongue cling to the roof of my mouth
    if I do not remember you,
if I do not consider Jerusalem
    my highest joy!
PSALM 137:1-6

The king was shaken. He went up to his room over the gateway and wept. As he went, he said: "O my son Absalom! My son, my son Absalom! If only I had died instead of you – O Absalom, my son, my son!"

    Joab was told, "The King is weeping and mourning for Absalom."
And for the whole army the victory that day was turned into mourning,

because on that day troops heard it said,
"The king is grieving for his son."
2 SAMUEL 18:33–19:2

THE EXILES IN BABYLON had lost a city and home; King David had lost a son. The grieving they experienced was similar. All loss involves grieving whether it is loss of a person, a possession, a job, a settled way of life, a loss of home, of status. And all grieving over time involves a mixture: waves of emotion, from numbness and denial to anger, despair and a sense of emptiness. The creative springs dry up. Any change will involve some loss, and in a fast changing world we are consciously or unconsciously constantly mourning the world we have known and of which we have been a part.

In these words perhaps you are overwhelmingly conscious of a source of grief. The experiences of the exiles and David are almost too close, too direct to bear. On the other hand there may not be something specific but you can identify with a sense of regret, of sadness when you are still. One of the ways in which we cope with grief at a very basic level is by losing ourselves in business, activity and routine. Preparations for funerals serve this purpose; so do the packed diaries of those who have retired. By hurrying, by rushing we not only try to prevent our own grief coming to the surface and overwhelming us; we also give signals to others that there is no time to share our grief.

In contemporary society we have created greater speed. We often seem incapable of letting our souls catch up with our fast-moving bodies. We tend to split off our feelings and grief. This is not just a question of individuals finding it hard to grieve because of personal loss but the grieving of the whole of a community or society – a collective denial of, or failure to be in touch with, corporate loss.

If we cannot grieve then life presents us with unending reminders of the original cause of our grieving and the need to deny our pain becomes increasingly pressing. A vicious circle is established. But if we are brave enough to be still, if God forces us to be still, then grieving can occur and the healing that is the close companion of grieving will slip in beside us. We will find ourselves able to respond to new situations and challenges without past loss casting dark shadows over every experience.

And how can we grieve in a way that is not neurotic and dysfunctional? It is about being, not doing. There can be no effective do-it-yourself manual of grieving, but there is the collective wisdom of centuries to enlighten us when we are ready. One insight is not to run away; to deny. It is important to stay with the loss and the emotional responses. In some cultures and societies this is easier than others. The responses may be unpredictable, even chaotic, but they are to be welcomed rather than feared, shared rather than locked away.

For those who worship regularly real feelings can be brought into a place, into a setting, where they are accepted. They are not to be left outside and collected again when the worship is over, but to be brought to the foot of the cross. Our Saviour, who is such a loving shepherd and wise counsellor, will not only accept but welcome us as we are, in our brokenness or confusion. Some years ago when I was going through a period of grieving and anxiety, I slipped unnoticed into a cathedral for a weekday communion service. The liturgy was simple and well-known, but what I experienced above all else was the solidity, the strength, of the building itself. I was within a place where generations had come with every manner of problem, sin and grief. Yet here it was still, a silent testimony to the lasting nature of faith. It would be there after my crisis. And so it is that we can bring our grief to the Lord, for he is strong enough to accept us as we are.

We all have those images, and know people and passages of Scripture that represent the security of God's love, in many ways that we treasure. Many find comfort in hymns such as those that speak of "the everlasting arms", of the grace of Christ. *Great is thy faithfulness* tells of one who can "hold" us whatever our problems or personal crises. The significant thing is not that we say anything, or hear anything, but that we find ourselves being in God's presence, silently drawing strength and comfort from his enfolding.

This may or may not involve people, whether family, friends, or counsellors. Each of these can be ways in which God can demonstrate his everlasting love to us. Equally we may find it is alone where our grief is shared and embraced. We will probably need others with whom we can share some of the time, but certainly not all of the time. And through this we will discover we are not alone in our grieving and loss. They will be with us, not talking to us or counselling us, for they understand what it is to grieve enough to know that words so often fail and mar ....

But healthy grieving that is not a regression or flight from reality always takes place in the context of knowing that life is to be faced, challenges are to be renewed. The grieving state is not for ever. And in this way there is the recognition that the loss is not the whole picture (however much it might feel that way). There will be an oscillation of state of mind but grieving is something we pass through, not the end and destination of our journey.

The positive aspect of the experience of grief is the fact that something, or someone, has been precious enough to cause us so great a sense of loss. No doubt an aspect of this is the wish and the dream but behind there is the reality, however distant, however distorted by emotions. That sounds like cold comfort but it is to be pondered. Over my years in residential care I have known some children who have no conscious awareness of losing anything – there seem to have been no bonds or relationships which have been lost and are regretted. Their resources for dealing with future crises are extremely limited. The point is that what causes the grief can also in time bring comfort. But nothing is to be rushed, nothing denied, nothing predicted. We are to stay in touch with our grief: to be. The rest will follow. God has a myriad ways of replicating the massive reliability of the cathedral walls as we bring our confusion and loss to him.

PRAYERS

"Lord,
    It's just so unpredictable. Emotions come in waves. And the
    loss and change go so deep, affect so much of me, I'm not at all

sure life will go on in any normal way again. So many people
and situations bring tears to my eyes ...."

"Child,
You're cradled in my arms; you're held; you're safe. Don't fret
about whether you're 'getting better' or whether you will return
to 'normal'. In my way and in my time springtime will replace
the cold winter of your experience. It will bring its own pain as
numbness recedes. But be, for now. Your loss is also your
strength, for that which you have lost belonged to you, and in a
deeper way, still belongs to you. And you, my child, belong to
me."

5. Resting

*He carried into exile to Babylon the remnant who escaped from the
sword, and they became servants to him and his sons until the kingdom
of Persia came to power. The land enjoyed its sabbath rests; all the time
of its desolation it rested, until the seventy years were completed in
fulfilment of the word of the LORD spoken by Jeremiah.*
2 CHRONICLES 36:20-21

*One day Jesus said to his disciples, "Let's go over to the other side of the
lake." So they got into a boat and set out. As they sailed, he fell asleep.
A squall came down on the lake, so that the boat was being swamped,
and they were in great danger. The disciples went and woke him, ...*
LUKE 8:22-24

THE STORY OF JESUS resting in a boat tossing in the storm is well-
known. He had entered into a deep sleep which was so needed
because of his arduous ministry. The last chapter of 2 Chronicles
is virtually unknown, yet it has so much to teach. The long-feared invasion
and destruction of Jerusalem has finally taken place. The people are led
away into exile and the disaster predicted by the prophets has occurred. It
was a tragedy of vast proportions and horrific intensity, given all the
history of Israel and the Promised Land. Significantly when Moses spoke

his last words to the people centuries before he warned about just such a scattering and he described it as the exact opposite of rest and resting.

> *"Among those nations you will find no repose, no resting place for the sole of your foot. There the LORD will give you an anxious mind, eyes weary with longing, and a despairing heart. You will live in constant suspense."*
> DEUTERONOMY 28:65-66

That is the side of the narrative we identify with: we follow the exiles into captivity. But the passage from Chronicles looks at a completely different aspect of the exile. It surveys the land promised to Israel and now largely deserted. For generations it has suffered because of the disobedience and sin of God's people. They have flouted his commands and deserved his curses. Sadly as in the story of Genesis, when humans sin it has an effect on the rest of the natural world. Now at last the land enjoys the rest it had been waiting for so long: it has seventy years of sabbath rests. Biblically-speaking sabbaths are all about rest and re-creation: they are the meantime between two weeks of activity, when there is time and space to review the past and anticipate the future.

In the contemporary world opportunities for such rest, individually or corporately, are becoming rarer. We live at a time, often characterised as "24/7", when there is human restlessness possibly unparalleled in human history. On the other hand we know the importance of rest for healing, growth and well-being. That last word is so special in the context of this book: well-being. Rest is obviously not about activity or doing, and it is one of the aspects of being we can all understand, at least in theory. Convalescing and healing are essentially about resting. Once the operation has taken place, the medicine or treatment has been given, there is that vital period of rest. It means time off work and a new pattern of life. It may require a time in bed, a time in comparative isolation. Treatment may be made more effective and can be sped up. But rest must take its own course. It's about experiencing new rhythms and patterns. Sleep is a case in point. The whole body assumes new rhythms during a restful sleep. Breathing and heartbeats slow; the unconscious begins to become dominant and dreams occur. And this (as with Jesus in the boat) is both a constituent part, and also a symbol, of convalescence, healing and rest.

In reflecting on the subject of rest I've been taking time out of a conference in order to be on the Malvern Hills in Worcestershire. Mostly I've reflected alone – on quiet walks to the Worcester Beacon, North Hill and south towards the Hereford Beacon. But I've also shared with one or two people asking for their comments and digesting their experiences and insights. One common theme began to emerge: it was in the natural world that the healing rhythms are most apparent. One person, looking up at the autumnal slopes of the hills that had so inspired Elgar, was deeply struck by the way they contrasted with inner cities and urban living. It was not just that the scenery was different but that there was a rest for the soul she could not find in the ceaseless activity of city life (both its exciting and also its depressing sides).

That is something poets, artists and mystics have discovered through the ages. The natural world is not static. It is not predictable in every respect. But beneath the surface the almost imperceptible daily, weekly and seasonal pulse-beats give evidence of life and relationships at a pace so different from our own. It's not surprising that so many sanatoria, striking for their natural presence and beauty, have sprung up in parts of the world; that people have literally tried to apply (mud cures), immerse themselves in (hot springs) and digest (freshwater springs) the natural world. These are all indications of our collective recognition of the rest and healing to be found among the woods, hills, streams, seas and fields of the natural world.

One of the contributions of the Romantic movement was to suggest ways in which humans could become one with the natural world. Byron put it with his effortless clarity:

> "Are not the mountain seas and skies
> Part of me and of my soul, as I of them?"

The mystery is profound, but we know that such identification does not come from photographing nature, climbing mountains, collecting samples and souvenirs. It comes from resting in nature. It is about being –

sometimes still, sometimes gently moving with nature itself, adjusting to the stillness and movement of nature. Those who rise with the sunrise and rest with the sunset, who notice the patterns of ebbing tides, the gathering of the migrating birds, the ripening of fruit on mossed apple trees, have already begun that process of rest and accommodation with nature.

In turn nature itself is respected and, in some measure, understood. So we come back to the place where we started. If we set up human systems over and against nature we are likely to pollute and defile it. As we come to respect nature then we not only experience rest but also pass it on, unconsciously, to the natural world. This is, in essence, the Old Testament's teaching about the relationship between people and the land.

Being in nature and with it is not about possession, domination, ownership, but about acceptance and being accepted. And it's not about assuming nature is always rosy. Today on the Malvern Hills the bedraggled rosebay willowherb had died, the trees had shed many of their leaves. Winter with its harsh winds and bleak days and long nights was heralded. That is not in any way depressing or worrying. The hills have experienced countless such seasons. As night falls the stars wheel overhead, the dawn is not far behind and winter will be followed by spring. It is not hurried or capable of speeding up or slowing down. We are either part of it or cut off from it.

There are those who have known true rest in prison cells or city streets. But those who have the choice know instinctively that, in touch with nature, we discover the rest that reaches into our souls.

PRAYERS

"Lord,
Forgive my restlessness. I don't choose it all. It's not simply an escape through busyness. Help me to be in touch with your creation, your pulse-beat, your walking pace. May I rest in your presence surrounded by your handiwork."

"Child,

This is isn't an easy request you make, for your society travels too fast. It is cut off from the wisdom and patterns of centuries embedded in natural rhythms. Don't be sentimental and long for faraway places. Start here and now, today. Are there stars overhead? Is there a wren in that bush? Are there falling leaves on that tree? And if all else fails don't forget the sky … the heavens as some used to call it. Perhaps they were nearer than modern translators realised. Relax and be. Don't worry about meaning or understanding … being, well-being … rest … sabbath … The deepest sleep is often found during the biggest storms."

6. Surviving

Some time later, Benhadad king of Aram mobilised his entire army and marched up and laid siege to Samaria. There was a great famine in the city; the siege lasted so long that a donkey's head sold for eighty shekels of silver, and a quarter of a cab of seed pods for five shekels. As the king of Israel was passing by on the wall, a woman cried to him, "Help me, my lord the king!" The king replied "If the LORD does not help you, where can I get help for you? From the threshing-floor? From the wine-press?" Then he asked her, "What's the matter?" She answered, "This woman said to me, 'Give up your son so that we may eat him today, and tomorrow we'll eat my son.' So we cooked my son and ate him. The next day I said to her, 'Give up your son so that we may eat him,' but she had hidden him." When the king heard the woman's words, he tore his robes. As he went along the wall, the people looked, and there, underneath, he had sackcloth on his body ....
2 KINGS 6:24-30

"To the angel of the church in Smyrna write: 'These are the words of him who is the First and the Last, who died and came to life again. I know your afflictions and your poverty – yet you are rich! I know the slander of those who say they are Jews and are not, but are a synagogue of Satan. Do not be afraid of what you are about to suffer. I tell you, the devil will put some of you in prison to test you, and you will suffer persecution for

ten days. Be faithful, even to the point of death, and I will give you the crown of life.'"
REVELATION 2:8-10

SIEGES LIKE BENHADAD'S have been more common in history than we care to think and they are crueller than we can bear to imagine. If we want to read about survival we prefer stories of great adventures on mountains, across deserts or on the seas. One of the great twentieth century stories of survival that has become a classic in more ways than one is the record of the family whose yacht was sunk by a whale in the Pacific. The title is carefully chosen: *Survive the Savage Sea*, in order to distinguish between surviving and hoping for a rescue. Survival in essence must be done without hope of any outside intervention.

We find it hard to accept that for many millions of people on earth at this very moment life is characterised by a struggle for survival in the face of war, disease and famine. There are thousands of children in refugee camps and cities, whose thoughts are not turned towards what they want to be when they grow up, but on how they are to survive another twenty-four hours.

If we have not personally experienced such long-term and physically acute struggles it may well be that we have endured emotional and spiritual periods when survival rather than growth or progress has dominated our horizons. The church at Smyrna knew this as a group. It is not that the situation is desirable or that survival is an accurate description of all that happens, especially from God's point of view or with hindsight; it is simply to recognise that from our point of view we are conscious only of the struggle for survival.

It may be after a relationship has ended, broken by death or a change of mind or commitment, after a job is lost, or after an accident, that we can only go through the motions of life for a time. We might like to rise above it, see beyond it, but we can't and we don't. We are simply holding on. It may be that as you read this you can think of one or more periods when survival was your main priority. It may be you are going through such an experience here and now. At such times no sermon or story with a moral is likely to help. Everything seems so futile, and so distant. Strangely enough, comfort and encouragement may be nearer than we realise.

It starts with the recognition and acceptance that survival is a real issue. It doesn't deride the struggle for experience of survival as second best or unacceptable. It doesn't seek to deny the pain of the struggle, nor what has led to it. It doesn't present a picture of an immediate accessible light at the end of the tunnel. Instead there is a coming alongside and an experiencing of that struggle in its reality. It involves solidarity and sharing. For there may be no obvious escape: the reality may be that a person or group has no other viable option. As the reality is understood, the bravery of the struggle becomes appreciated. The survivor is, by definition, not someone who has given up. Many have done, perhaps all are tempted to, but the survivor is not among them. Survivors accept the inescapable realities of a situation and still hold on. It is about "being" in a very definite and practical sense. It is not about planning a way out, for that way does not exist, but it is about choosing to be, not to capitulate or to give up. It is about daily routine and patterns.

The story of the hostages in Beirut during the 1980s has been told and retold. It is compulsive reading, partly because there was individually and collectively a will to survive, manifest not in great faith and great gestures, but in the minutest details of everyday life. Conversation, exercises, meals (such as they were) all disciplined because built on that rock of survival. In shared captivity the solidarity was at the most poignant.

The recognition of the bravery of the survivor inevitably leads on to the acceptance that there is something above and beyond the inescapable situation that is worth living for. There is a person, a job, a place that draws us to think ourselves outside of the captivity that will not let us give up hope and despair. To understand why some prisoners of war and concentration camps survived but others didn't, Victor Frankl discovered the basis of his own form of psychiatry - logotherapy. The survivors all had a reason to live beyond the prison camp: there were those who needed them, there was work to do. There was something within them that would not let them lie down and accept a decline leading to death.

In this way surviving with its acceptance of limitations, and with its narrow horizons, is also about a quality of life and being. The New Testament often talks about "holding on", "holding fast" and "being faithful". The situation is often stark and bleak. The Christians, and churches like those of Smyrna, are being persecuted by the might of the Roman Empire. They are urged not to give up. And what is it that stirs them, that provides courage to face each day against seemingly impossible odds? It is that vision of Jesus, the Lamb who has died and is alive for evermore; the voice of his calling; the future celebration and worship around his throne, knowing that "for the joy set before him (he) endured the cross" (Hebrews 12:2).

PRAYERS

"Lord,
I know you didn't mean it, but those last words sound like the beginning of a sermon. The reality is that sometimes everything in my life is geared to survival: nothing more, nothing less. I have no time, no energy for anything else. I just want to know that you understand what I'm going through, what others are going through."

"Child,
I know how it feels to you, really I do, but there is another side to your struggle for survival. Whether you like it or not Paul was right: 'suffering produces perseverance, perseverance character, and character, hope'. I can see that perseverance in you, while you perceive only the struggle. You must hold on, you will hold on, and though you cannot understand it or accept it I am holding you and no one will pluck you out of my hand.

   Understanding will come later, and most likely not through sermons ...."

7. Contemplating

The LORD said to Job:

"Will the one who contends with the Almighty correct him?
Let him who accuses God answer him!"

Then Job answered the LORD:

"I am unworthy – how can I reply to you?
I put my hand over my mouth.
I spoke once, but I have no answer –
twice but I will say no more....

My ears had heard of you
but now my eyes have seen you."
JOB 40:1-5; 42:5

"For the Lamb at the centre of the throne will be their shepherd; he will
lead them to springs of living water. And God will wipe away every tear
from their eyes." When he opened the seventh seal, there was silence in
heaven for about half an hour.
REVELATION 7:17–8:1

THE TWO BEAUTIFULLY precise descriptions of silence contrast with the importance we attach to words, speech and sound in all human situations, sacred and secular. Communication is often made possible by them, whether written, spoken or relayed by information technology. Just think of the thousands of radio stations, tapes, newspapers, magazines, pens, typewriters, PC's, mobile and cell phones relentlessly pouring out their verbal messages right now! Words are important in our own personal development and understanding. Equally they play an axiomatic role in the development of the Christian faith in creeds, songs, sacred writings, testimonies and theology itself.

But there is, there has to be a place, a space for silence, pure, unadulterated silence. This means quiet, detached stillness, and, in its purest form, the absence of thoughts and pictures. One of the differences between meditation and contemplation is that the former starts with a person, an object, a situation, an idea and reflects on it in the light of God's love until it is recast, remoulded, understood in a new way and a new context. Michel Quoist's *Prayers of Life* are a special aid to meditation in everyday life.

Contemplation, on the other hand, will start with a passage of Scripture, a picture, a situation, and move into a state of being where pictures, words and thoughts are left behind and transcended. It is about a movement towards God and thinking about him; a regard of God accompanied by love which results in a heightened awareness of his presence and his nature. It is a penetration of the spiritual world, an experience of perfect insight, not mediated by anything, because the veils that separate us from God have been parted. We know we are in his presence, communing with him.

We can perhaps apply what Wordsworth wrote in his *Lines written above Tintern Abbey* to this process:

> *... the motion of our human blood*
> *Almost suspended; we are laid asleep*
> *In body, and become a living soul:*
> *While with an eye made quiet with the power*

> Of humanity and the deep power of joy
> We see into the life of things.

The book of Job recounts a prolonged conversation focused on Job's suffering: its causes and meaning. Until God's revelation of himself at the end it is presumed that some explanation can be found with the words and thoughts. In fact Job's experience of the living God transcends everything. He is reduced to silence having seen the living God. It is not that the questions have been answered in words, but that God's presence has replaced questions, discussion and answers. Job has been imagining an advocate who would intercede on his behalf before God. Now Job is overwhelmed by God's presence, and everything else that might come between them is of no consequence or relevance. Perhaps the wisest things his would-be counsellors did was to sit with him for seven days and nights (Job 2:11-13) without saying a word. There is suffering, there is joy, there is experience and communion that lies too deep, too intense, too real for words, and this is Job's discovery.

In the Book of Revelation the focus of all is the Lamb who sits at the centre of the throne. This is the culmination of history, the climax of the symphony which God has been writing and conducting from the beginning of time. Images and ideas are born and reborn. (Austin Farrer's *Glass of Vision* is a wonderful exploration of this process). Layer upon layer of meaning is added. And the result? Silence in heaven. As the writer of Ecclesiastes put it, "For everything there is a time to speak and a time to be silent" (Ecclesiastes 3:7). And the experience of contemplation is one when only silence will do. Prayer, worship and adoration are gathered into the silence which seems to crash over you, to suspend time and transcend space.

One of the parts of Scripture that helps an understanding of the essence of contemplation is the transfiguration of Jesus (see Mark 8:27–9:29). As a tool for beginning to enter into the nature of contemplation it is, perhaps, without parallel. The disciples Peter, James and John enter into a completely new awareness of the nature of Jesus, his relationship with the Law and the Prophets, and with God himself. Words fail. There is simply the longing that the experience might last for ever, for this is the heart of things. With time and training "our reading of the Gospel story can and should be an act of personal communion with the living God" (William Temple: *Readings in St. John's Gospel*).

Such experiences are neither common nor straightforward. They require discipline and training. There is usually a group or family with whom the preparation takes place. A tradition is necessary for most, and rhythm and patterns are a vital way in; the physical setting and posture all matter. Occasionally we are surprised by a moment of insight and truth when we see that everything coheres in Christ, that "all shall be well". Such moments and disclosures are God-given and usually cannot be anticipated. Yet in regular worship the elements necessary come together especially at the communion/eucharist/mass. For as the bread and wine are digested into our bodies, so we become part of the divine and he is part of us (Christ in us and we in Christ). The process is notable for its hiddenness and silence. Words are irrelevant at this point.

PRAYERS

"Lord,
There are those who have seen you so clearly, loved you so dearly and followed you so nearly. I know I've such a long way to go in my pilgrimage. The heroes of Scripture like Isaiah and John inspire me as do those in the church like St. John of the Cross, Mother Julian of Norwich, John Bunyan, Thomas Merton. Yet to be frank it can all be a little bit depressing."

"Child,
Your body is a temple of the Holy Spirit. Yes, yours. No more and no less that those you have listed, not to mention the thousands of others known only to me, who have been and are one with me, without anyone else knowing. Our conversation here and now shows how far you have already travelled. Why

not forget others, those you admire and start becoming more aware of yourself, of your body, of your church family and traditions. You are the temple in which I meet with you, I have met with you and I will be with you. Why not feed on me in the centre of your temple by faith with thanksgiving? Let's not get into a debate or conversation. Why not be still, be silent. You have no distance to travel, no mountains to climb. I've done all that. Let's be quiet together. Yes, you and me."

8. Waiting

"Not one of you will enter the land I swore with uplifted hand to make your home, except Caleb son of Jephuneh and Joshua son of Nun. As for your children that you said would be taken as plunder, I will bring them in to enjoy the land you have rejected. ... Your children will be shepherds here for forty years, suffering for your unfaithfulness, until the last of your bodies lies in the desert."

NUMBERS 14:30-31,33

How long, O LORD? Will you forget me for ever?
      How long will you hide your face from me?
How long must I wrestle with my thoughts
      and every day have sorrow in my heart?
      How long will my enemy triumph over me?
Look on me and answer, O LORD my God.
      Give light to my eyes, or I will sleep in death;
my enemy will say, I have overcome him,
      and my foes will rejoice when I fall.

But I trust in your unfailing love;
      my heart rejoices in your salvation.
I will sing to the LORD, for he has been good to me."

PSALM 13

One who was there had been an invalid for thirty-eight years.
When Jesus saw him lying there and learned that he had been in this
condition for a long time, he asked him, "Do you want to get well?"
"Sir," the invalid replied, "I have no one to help me into the pool ... "
JOHN 5:5-7

IN EVERYDAY LIFE at home there are little periods of waiting – for the kettle to boil or the toast to brown, for the bread to rise, for someone to answer the phone, for the postman to come. Outside our homes there are those times at supermarket checkouts, at bus queues, on stations, at airports, or in traffic jams and at traffic lights. At work, however well organised, there are waits: for the photocopier, for the delivery, for something to dry or set. Then there are longer periods of waiting – for exam results, for diagnosis following a test or scan, for news of an interview, for a relationship to develop, for crops to ripen.

Such periods of waiting, small and great, are also experienced by groups, including families, organisations, churches, communities or nations. A family awaits the birth or death of one of its members, waits for an offer on its house; an organisation awaits news of an impending takeover; a church waits to hear about a new minister; a community waits for the result of its objection to a new by-pass; a nation waits for the end of war or famine.

The waiting of groups and individuals are, of course, inextricably linked, and in the case of the Israelites waiting for forty years to enter the Promised Land it was Joshua and Caleb who probably needed most patience. They had entered the land with other spies and recommended invasion. They were outvoted and so spent forty years wandering through the wilderness waiting for the moment they knew would come – one to be a leader, the other to receive his reward. It must have been a particularly frustrating and trying period for them. And we know that it was just so for the whole community, from the number of times they looked back with nostalgia towards old times in Egypt.

Often we wait alone as individuals rather than as part of a group. The man who had sat for thirty-eight years beside the pool at Bethsaida was one who watched others healed but who waited alone, unnoticed and in vain. For him waiting had become such an ingrained part of his existence that it's not clear he was really waiting for anything at all. Hence the question of Jesus "Do you want to get better?"

At certain life stages and in certain situations we become those who wait. Retirement is just such a period. Not simply or predominantly waiting for death, becoming more dependent on others and their priorities and routines, especially the family. The unemployed also know about waiting: being reliant on others, being inactive, being forced to wait for news of another interview or job. Being ill is one of the purest forms of waiting. We become patients. One moment active, the next passive: the recipients of the care, the decisions, the treatment of others. If we are very ill we literally wait on others for everything, from the drip, to the food, to the bedpan.

We have seen that our contemporary western society stresses the value of activity, of busyness, business and activity, specified objectives and tangible outcome. The puritan work ethic is deeply embedded in our conscious and unconscious attitudes. Increasingly leisure is conceived as something active, holidays, travel, classes for everything, plenty of planned activity. School holidays for many children mean camps, courses and planned activities. A happy retirement is supposed to be an active one, with at least one cruise to an exotic part of the world. Happiness equals activity. Partly to compensate for the long spells watching television, but also to reflect on the virtue of action, movement and doing.

This means that becoming a patient, becoming unemployed, facing retirement is all the more difficult: any period of waiting becomes almost unbearably frustrating for many people. Yet it is in waiting that we are often at our most observant, aware and human. W.H. Vanstone made a study of the gospels of Mark and John which is summarised in his book *The Stature of Waiting*. In it he records how Jesus, the man of love, the man of action, the preacher and the healer, becomes at an exact moment in the Garden of Gethsemane the man who waits, the man who is handed over, the man whom others handle and treat. The one who has all power becomes of his own free will the one who is the object of the decisions of others.

It is, like all Vanstone's writing, strikingly original. For in this way Jesus enters into that aspect of human condition that is so real, so prevalent for each of us. We are not in control of our own destiny: we must await the will of others and processes outside our own domain. But the heart of the book and the heart of the whole issue is this: in that period of waiting, of passivity, there is something of what it is to be fully human. There is a stature in waiting. There is insight, receptivity, awareness, a depth of relationship with others and the world itself, not found and known in action. It is part of the process by which relationships can be transformed from "I - it" relationships to "I - thou" relationships.

In the life of action and activity, things and others are seen as objects, as entities: they are counted, talked with, moved, shaped. As we wait we can see and experience the world in a new light. We can understand and recognise dimensions and connections that remain hidden in the active mode. We can receive much more than the healing facilitated by medical treatment or the help of others: something from the heart of things, of beauty, truth and goodness.

PRAYERS

"Lord,
That all sounds very well, but it seems to underestimate the sheer frustration I feel in waiting, and the destructiveness of illness, unemployment and retirement. Lots of people can't bear it and don't come through. It isn't a positive experience for everyone. But by faith I will try and see waiting as an experience that isn't wholly negative."

"Child,
You know that I know how you feel. Gethsemane, the hand over by Judas, the trials and the minutes waiting for the cross

to be put in place. But it was in that period that I received the hurt and pain of others, the sins of the world, and through that reality that healing, light, forgiveness came. Please don't underestimate how hard it was. Theologians are still fretting over the words, 'My God, my God, why have you forsaken me.' What they rarely seem to understand is that this moment of time was an eternity of waiting."

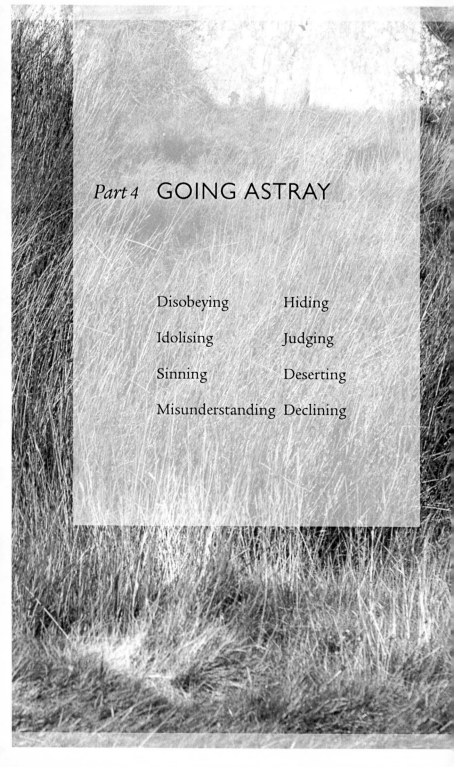

Part 4 GOING ASTRAY

Disobeying   Hiding

Idolising   Judging

Sinning   Deserting

Misunderstanding Declining

MOST TEENAGERS brought up in a Christian context probably sooner or later realise that the sermon they're listening to is vaguely similar to one they've heard before, that they have sung these hymns and songs many times, that worship however creative or rich is repetitive. If we know it (all?) then why do we go to worship week after week? There are many ways of responding but the most immediate and telling is our need to confess our sins and failings before God, to seek his cleansing and renewal. The picture of human beings like a flock of sheep is particularly apt in this respect. For it is the nature of a sheep to wander in search of fresh grass. Thus "straying" is probably more often unconscious than conscious, and is as true of the herd as of the individual sheep or lamb.

We may like to pretend we don't often make mistakes or fall far short of God's standards, but deep within we know differently. There are theologies where the stress on the total depravity of the human race and the individual seems oppressive in worship or teaching. They are surely nearer the mark than theologies which shy away from any hint of human sin and wickedness. But the most honest and integrated approach is to accept the tendency to stray as a fact of life and to find ways of responding to it and dealing with it that are healthy and helpful. If every slip provokes a sense of crisis, fear and despair, ordinary life will cease to be possible (as many mental hospitals or unhappy offspring can testify). If no slip is recognised then life becomes normless and rudderless. The net effect over time may be very little different leading to something resembling individual or corporate neurosis.

The reality of sin in God's world is a fact that every generation has to face and with which it must wrestle. Scripture itself, if seen from this perspective, is a vast treatise on this very subject. A perfect world is marred by sin, but God in his grace and love enters into it in order to redeem and restore it. This is one of the central themes from Genesis to Revelation. If we hold on to the "why?" of all this then a mysterious and deep truth begins to emerge from under the rubble. There is something gained when a sheep is lost and found again that was not present before. There is a cause for celebration. A relationship has not only been restored but enriched in the process. This is no excuse or reason for sinning (as Paul vigorously pointed out in Romans in response to the question, "Shall we sin that grace may abound?"), but it may help us begin to fathom why in God's sovereignty a world capable of so much sin, hatred and straying was better than no world at all.

When sharing this section of the book with trusted friends, at least one suggested that I drop this section. They told me that it was far too close to the wind theologically. I have pondered this advice but, as you can see, I persevered with it. The reason is this: without it we cannot have a representative sample of themes. The meantime consists not just of good, but of bad. And yet God is working through all things. And what's more this section gives the reader the opportunity to be real about ways in which he or she has fallen short, and to seek forgiveness. This is not about grand sins of the scale of David when he murdered one of his officers in order to cover up his adultery with Bathsheba, or of Judas when he betrayed his Lord. It is about the sins that so easily beset us everyday.

1. Disobeying

When Jeremiah finished telling the people all the words of the LORD their God – everything the LORD had sent him to tell them – Azariah son of Hoshaiah and Johanan son of Kareah and all the arrogant men said to Jeremiah, "You are lying! The LORD our God has not sent you to say, 'You must not go to Egypt to settle there.' But Baruch son of Neriah is inciting you against us to hand us over to the Babylonians, so that they may kill us or carry us into exile to Babylon."

So Johanan son of Kareah and all the army officers and all the people disobeyed the LORD's command to stay in the land of Judah. ... So they entered Egypt in disobedience to the LORD.
JEREMIAH 43:1-3;7A

God ... gave them over to a depraved mind, to do what ought not to have been done. They have become filled with every kind of wickedness, evil, greed and depravity. They are full of envy, murder, strife, deceit and malice. They are gossips, slanderers, God-haters, insolent, arrogant and boastful; they invent ways of doing evil; they disobey their parents; they are senseless, faithless, heartless, ruthless. Although they know God's righteous decree that those who do such things deserve death, they not only continue to do these very things but also approve of those who practise them.
ROMANS 1:28-32

For just as through the disobedience of the one man the many were made sinners, so also through the obedience of the one man the many will be made righteous.
ROMANS 5:19

D ISOBEDIENCE IS PROBABLY the primal form of sin. The young child is told what to do and what not to do in very black and white terms. The rules are mostly concerned with safety and survival – don't touch the fire, don't put that worm or insect in your mouth, don't pick up that knife and so on. As we know, not only from Paul as quoted above, but also from many commentators including Milton in his great epic *Paradise Lost*:

> *Of Man's first disobedience, and the fruit*
> *Of that forbidden tree, whose mortal taste*
> *Brought death into the world, and all our woe ...*

this is the start. It is a wilful refusal to do what we ought to do, or to refrain from what we ought not to do. For this reason the confessional prayer in worship all over the world includes just such a phrase.

The fundamental task of a prophet is to spell out the truth, to confront people with choices and the need for repentance. Because of the human propensity for disobedience this has always meant the role and lot of the prophet has been an unenviable one. If they are faithful in proclaiming their message they are bound to be despised or marginalised at some point in their career. Jeremiah is the archetypal prophet because of his absolutely fearless attitude whatever the odds. He resisted the temptation to dilute his message to make any audience like it.

If he had been speaking to us – to our church or group – we would have known exactly what he meant. Yet as we grow older and wiser we discover that things are not always quite as black and white as the issue separating Jeremiah from Johanan. It is not always obvious what obedience to God's law requires. For a start those who are clear in telling us what to do may have their own motives, conscious or unconscious; then there are many situations in which it is not at all clear what the right course of action (the "ought") really is. Notions of obedience and disobedience seem relics of a child's world and worldview. Aren't we old enough to create our own codes of conduct for our particular contemporary culture and context?

There is no easy way out of this dilemma as philosophers, theologians, politicians and psychiatrists can all testify from their distinctive perspectives and experiences. But we don't need external confirmation of our own personal moral struggles. Paul spoke for us all when he admitted that he was unable to do what he knew he ought to do and was unable to resist what was wrong (Romans 7:21-25). If there are lessons to be learned from history, one could be that a society which takes the moral law into its own hands heads for disaster. Consider the appalling tragedies of Stalinist Russia, Pol Pot's Cambodia, Hitler's Germany and Maoist China in the twentieth century before arguing too strongly for laws and patterns of life dictated by specific historical and cultural factors. (And we dare not, as Salman Rushdie so incisively remarked in *The Moor's Last Sigh*, simply write these leaders off as monsters. We are all more implicated in these tragedies than we care to believe.)

So where do we go given the twin pillars of the Judaeo-Christian moral code ("Love the Lord your God with all your heart, soul, mind and strength" and "Love your neighbour as yourself") on the one hand, and the complexities of the human condition on the other? The evidence seems to be that though we ought to be able to work out what is right and what is wrong, in fact we cannot. And even if we can work it out individually or collectively, we still find it alarmingly easier to disobey our deepest consciences and moral instincts.

In my ministry from church to church and denomination to denomination I find that even the most mature people and fellowships find members doing what is wrong and spoiling what is good. I recall sitting outside a church one summer Sunday after leading worship. A member of the congregation had asked to speak with me. "I have been married twice and divorced, but now I have found the right person. Some members of the fellowship are cautious. Will you confirm that God is a forgiving God and that it is right to start again?" The whole tenor and tone of what he said revealed the elementary need for firm boundaries in his life – otherwise others would suffer as two previous wives had done. On another occasion after a seminar with clergy, one of the members of the group asked me "Is adultery always wrong?" Once again the need for a restatement of a clear boundary was being asked for. In the latter case the matter was resolved. I fear I don't know what happened in the former situation.

So after fifty years observing human life from within a residential community and neighbourhood, as a sociologist and as one who loves to scan world history and literature, I am bound to conclude that we need clear moral imperatives, agreements for any groups to function. That includes marriage and family, communities, firms and businesses, social institutions, markets, nations and federations of nations. Perhaps the late twentieth century and early twenty-first century passion for charters or bills of rights is an unconscious acknowledgement of this.

It means that there's no ducking out of the fundamental issue: to obey or to disobey?

If we believe we have grown up there is a tendency to begin to adapt precepts to our own advantage. Adulthood is no insurance against selfishness, wilfulness and wickedness. At root there are God-given principles and however much we might like to think we can derive them ourselves from personal and contemporary experience, we are prone to error. The purpose of these commandments, whatever it may seem to be, is actually to give us long and happy lives; that we might grow to adulthood. Those who are farthest on in the pilgrimage of faith are most acutely aware of the need for obedience to God's law.

PRAYERS

"Lord,
    In my heart I know what's right but in a post-modern world it's
    all getting rather confusing. So much consists of grey areas.
    Even so I have to admit that I know enough of my own

motivation and tendencies to realise I personally need clear moral precepts and all the help you can give me if I am to obey them."

"Child,

So much depends on your perspective, doesn't it? If one sees life and history as steady progress from childhood to adulthood then obedience seems out of place. But what if the rules are those that the wisest adults arrive at? And what if humans, whether children or adults, are all prone to wander? Are the fundamental laws of the universe any different for any particular group? 'All we like sheep have gone astray. We have turned every one to his own way.'"

2. Hiding

When the woman saw that the fruit of the tree was good for food and pleasing to the eye, and also desirable for gaining wisdom, she took some and ate it. She also gave some to her husband, who was with her, and he ate it. Then the eyes of both of them were opened, and they realised that they were naked; so they sewed fig leaves together and made coverings for themselves.

Then the man and his wife heard the sound of the LORD God as he was walking the garden in the cool of the day, and they hid from the LORD God among the trees of the garden. But the LORD God called to the man, "Where are you?"

He answered, "I heard you in the garden, and I was afraid because I was naked; so I hid."

GENESIS 3:6-10

"Woe to you, teachers of the law and Pharisees, you hypocrites! You are like whitewashed tombs, which look beautiful on the outside but on the inside are full of dead men's bones and everything unclean. In the same way, on the outside you appear to people as righteous but on the inside you are full of hypocrisy and wickedness."

MATTHEW 23:27-28

THE STORY IN GENESIS tells us that the immediate reaction of Adam and Eve after their disobedience was to hide. From then on it has ever been so. In a reflex action we try to cover up or hide a crime in order to avoid detection and punishment. But deeper than that is a sense of shame and betrayal – a wanting to deny that it ever happened at all. Ultimately, it's no use pretending: ordinary human life is full of attempts to hide or cover up the reality of wrongdoing, mistakes and miscalculations. Some are deeply thought out and formally planned, others pathetic in their ineffectiveness and conception. But no person or society can survive on the basis of a lie. A truly open and honest society would show how institutionalised the process of hiding is in our own. Let's leave aside the grand attempts to re-write history (the destruction of Nazi records and the constant attempts of rulers and governments to bury and destroy incriminating evidence like the Tiananmen Square massacre) and concentrate once again on the everyday process.

There are obvious reactions like lying and falsifying statements in all sorts of degrees from so-called "white lies" to gross distortions of the truth. And there is the literal hiding of evidence (the stolen goods hidden in a plastic bag, the pornographic magazine or book with a false cover, the flight of a murderer to another country). But in everyday life it is the taken-for-granted, subtle, insidious, institutionalised processes that are most powerful. Among them are the ideologies or false ideas that hide the real truth from groups of people. An example of this is the way in which religion, government and the media can portray a picture of wellbeing and progress which convinces unfortunate individuals and families (in their millions) that they are the unfortunate odd ones out as a result of their own failings and weaknesses. Churches and religions introduce such corporate myths in their own communities to hide true situations and motives to keep the pure truth from those on the margins.

Another process is the way in which we develop outward characteristics as human beings that mask our real identities. Jung talked of the personas we assume to compensate for the "shadows" within our personalities. (The shadow by the way is not to be identified with anything dark or evil, just the opposite of the revealed persona.) At their most obvious those who are uncertain of themselves project strengths; those who are nervous try to portray themselves as calm and so on. This mechanism is largely unconscious and so unexpected things upset our personas (perhaps a type of character or situation) because they have unsettled the balance between our persona and shadow. Another consequence is the problem that results in close relationships. A person is seeking a friend or partner that will complement their persona, but over time this can conflict with, and reveal, the shadow. Many broken marriages are the product of just this process. The received wisdom is of "mutual incompatibility". But why did the covenant relationship start with such high hopes and pledges? Our true selves remained hidden at great personal and social cost.

Then there is the crude but pervasive sin of hypocrisy. In seeking to get to the heart of the Law Jesus exposed in particular the hypocrisy of the Pharisees. But which of us can bear scrutiny in this respect? If our motives were known by everyone, if our innermost thoughts and private lives and actions were public knowledge where would we be? So much of what passes for charity, progressive policy and the like is at root a cover up. We are often most ardent public campaigners in areas of gravest personal and private weakness.

And the pettiness and processes can be extended. They encompass the busyness which hides personal failure and guilt; the projection of faults on to other individuals, parties, races, which hides personal failings; the crusading zeal which draws attention away from real issues; the stated values which mark actual realities (in practice how many men help equally with housework compared to those who say they do?) The failure to answer questions by politicians on the media has become almost legendary in its cynicism. But let us not start casting stones around. Hiding is part of our nature as much as clothing and fashion are part of our social life. It takes real bravery to expose oneself to the light of truth and genuine enquiry. Most of us prefer an unexplored murkiness and haze.

"Lord,
The implications of this are worrying for me personally and for social life in general. It's almost as if hiding is of epidemic proportions. How realistic is the desire for real openness in relationships?"

"Child,
Don't worry too much. The human reflexes for hiding are so well developed (defence mechanisms, some have called them) that there's not much danger of such openness. And in the wrong hands the very desire for genuine openness can be disastrous. It's just that if you are to get to know me better you will need to accept that there is no reason to hide anything. It isn't possible either. It's more about self-awareness than preaching. Humankind is unable to 'bear very much reality'."

3. Idolising

The Israelites said to Gideon, "Rule over us – you, your son and your grandson – because you have saved us out of the hand of Midian."

But Gideon told them, "I will not rule over you, nor will my son rule over you. The LORD will rule over you." And he said, "I do have one request, that each of you give me an ear-ring from your share of the plunder." ...

They answered, "We'll be glad to give them." So they spread out a garment, and each man threw a ring from his plunder onto it. The weight of the gold rings he asked for came to seventeen hundred shekels, not counting the ornaments, the pendants and the purple garments worn by the kings of Midian or the chains that were on their camels' necks. Gideon made the gold into an ephod, which he placed in Ophrah, his town. All Israel prostituted themselves by worshipping it there, and it became a snare to Gideon and his family.
JUDGES 8:22-27

To whom, then, will you compare God?
*   What image will you compare him to?*
As for an idol, a craftsman casts it,
*   and a goldsmith overlays it with gold*
*   and fashions silver chains for it.*
A man too poor to present such an offering

selects wood that will not rot.
He looks for a skilled craftsman
to set up an idol that will not topple.
ISAIAH 40:18-20

O NE OF THE FIRST PEOPLE to read the Narrative Bible all through had had nothing to do with church or the Christian religion before doing so. I was intrigued to know what he had discovered. His first comment was: "God doesn't like idolatry". And it doesn't take a very thorough or deep reading of the Scriptures to discover that the most commonly denounced sin is that of idolatry. It is named at the top of the list of the Ten Commandments and the warnings ring out from that moment on relentlessly. Sadly the incidence of idolatry is equally common especially in the historical books of Judges, Samuel, Kings and Chronicles. Whole epochs are summarised in terms of the attitude to idolatry displayed by rulers. The story of Gideon's leadership is well known: especially his destruction of idols, the fleece and his famous surprise victory with the reduced army of 300. Less well known is the end of his life where his ephod becomes an idol, and how things revert immediately after his death to idolatry once again.

Yet idolatry is described by Isaiah as silly. So why has it so captivated human minds and imaginations for most of history? We are made to be creative and one of our natural tendencies seems to be to create gods in our own image. They have come in virtually every size and shape. To have some visible manifestation that can be worshipped seems better than nothing and better even than the worship of the indescribable and invisible creator God of the Scriptures. Those who have come face to face with the living God through their community are no exception to this general tendency. However absurd the idols are to those looking on, however contradictory the myths associated with them they retain their hold. The story of Paul at Athens (Acts 17:16-31) illustrates the point nicely.

Once we get beyond thinking of idols simply as representations of gold, silver, wood and stone, the all-pervasive nature of idolatry becomes clear. It comprises everything that takes the worship due to God alone; anything that claims for itself and is credited with creative, healing, redemptive power other than God himself; anything that is worshipped and honoured above him. The truth is that given the whole world and the scope of human history everything seems to have attained this status at some time! Individuals have been deified, families and dynasties likewise, and reason, science, art, nation-states, techniques have all been put on pedestals and worshipped by some. There are holy places, holy times and holy people. No wonder sociologists looking at contemporary society find little evidence of a purely secular, rational world. Whatever else it is, it is not that.

Tragically, despite the Scriptures and the teaching of Jesus, Christianity has always tended to demonstrate just such a process. There are those who have worshipped the Church, the Pope, Saints, the Bible, great preachers, music, signs and wonders and liturgy in place of God himself. It has been said that some Protestants have replaced the Pope by a paper pope. This is not casting stones but indicating the pervasiveness of idolatry.

The tendency is so universal that one begins to see why it is so vigorously condemned in Scripture. It is anything but harmless. God has already given us his image, first in the creation of human beings (Genesis) and supremely in Jesus Christ. Anything that is created as an alternative image is not only false and inadequate but will eventually degrade the images God has already given. Eventually all idolatry degrades human beings and societies. They put themselves under caricatures and contortions of truth and become shaped by the very images they have themselves made. The great idols of contemporary society are reason, individualism disguised as democracy, progress and possessions. They are worshipped and great powers are attributed to them. When they fail they have not only disappointed they have derailed true worship. They have come between God and his creation.

When you hit upon the idol or idols of a person or society you find everything begins to fall into place in terms of explaining motivation, habits and values. But you have also touched a very sore spot. People will cling tenaciously to their idols like a child clutching his or her favourite doll. That's why the prayer of the famous hymn is so powerful and challenging:

The dearest idol I have known
Whate'er that idol be
Help me to tear it from thy throne
And worship only thee.

For idols don't just come ugly and stupid – they come as wonderful human beings, collectivism, great art and music. Anything can take God's place. There are no exceptions.

PRAYERS

"Lord,
I can see the truth of this so clearly in what I know of history and in other people and societies. What worries me is that I sense I'm bound to have blind spots just where I need the clearest vision! Given that as a human being I am prone to idolatry would you please help me to identify what the idols are, so that I may see all things as they are and relate to them and to you as I should?"

"Child,
I suggest you read one of the Gospels and put yourself in the shoes of the people Jesus met and challenged. When that happens you will be starting to get warm. For example how easy would you find it to sell all you have, to leave your career or family, to give up accepted customs and practices long held dear? If something seems easy to relinquish it is no idol. But in all this don't fall into the biggest trap of all: don't think more about idol-bashing than about me. That's so cruelly ironic."

4. Judging

"Do not judge, or you too will be judged. For in the same way as you judge others, you will be judged, and with the measure you use, it will be measured to you.

"Why do you look at the speck of sawdust in your brother's eye and pay no attention to the plank in your own eye? How can you say to your brother, 'Let me take the speck out of your eye,' when all the time there is a plank in your own eye? You hypocrite, first take the plank out of your own eye, and then you will see clearly to remove the speck from your brother's eye.

"Do not give to dogs what is sacred; do not throw your pearls to pigs. If you do, they may trample them under their feet, and then turn and tear you to pieces."
MATTHEW 7:1-6

Accept him whose faith is weak, without passing judgement on disputable matters. One man's faith allows him to eat everything, but another man, whose faith is weak, eats only vegetables. The man who eats everything must not look down on him who does not, and the man who does not eat everything must not condemn the man who does, for God has accepted him. Who are you to judge someone else's servant? To his own master he stands or falls. And he will stand, for the Lord is able to make him stand.
ROMANS 14:1-4

ONE OF MY UNIVERSITY teachers had the ability to sum up and analyse things very crisply. In our college chapel at Oxford he said of this passage from Matthew: "It teaches that we cannot be objective". I've pondered this since 1968 and it seems an excellent summary. It's obviously true: as human beings we are locked into our egos, our culture, backgrounds, and by the lack of our empathy and imagination unable to reach a god-like position or vantage point independent of bias and personal preferences and values.

Yet the fact is that we are always prone to judge the actions of others. We criticise other individuals, groups and cultures, directly and indirectly, specifically and implicitly, consciously and unconsciously. It may be that this is an essential element or our humanity: that we start from committed positions and traditions before we are ever aware of them.

The net result of this can be seen throughout history in some of those areas of the world where groups find it all but impossible to live and have a sense of identity without "others" whom they look down on and deem unreasonable, compromised and sometimes downright wrong. We can think immediately of the Hutu/Tutsi conflict in Uganda; the Protestant/Catholic divide in Northern Ireland; the Arab/Israeli conflict in the Middle East ... and the list is potentially endless.

But the tendency to judge is in evidence in the web of everyday life – in marriages, among peers, in communities, on the roads, in shops, schools and clubs. It's not just limited to the major theatres of conflict in the world ... and perhaps it was in ordinary life that the seeds of the sad and chronic conflicts were sown and took root.

Take something like travelling and crossing roads: as a pedestrian the motorists seem like road hogs; as a cyclist no one seems to notice you; as a driver all the traffic lights seem to favour the pedestrian and the cyclist! It all seems to depend on which you are doing and your vantage point.

Or take a meeting where decisions have to be taken (on a wider scale this would include a state election of course). There are quite different ways of doing this: formal agendas, resolutions and votes; friendly chats over a meal or a drink; African, European, American and Indian ways of discussing a matter and of coming to a conclusion. And it's so easy to judge the other ways of proceeding and assuming your own way is best.

We'd like to think that we can and do judge objectively, but that is beyond all but the saints, who claim they cannot! And when we appeal to supposedly objective standards, principles or worldviews these can be ideologically and politically shaped and biased.

And all the time what is happening is that our reactions, our comments, our criticisms, tell more about us and our context than they do about the matter or person we are judging. Years in India have taught me how tightly the colonial spectacles fit on me and how much they colour my vision; years being alongside women and children have taught me how the patriarchal bias infiltrates every relationship and evaluation.

And this is where Jesus and his observations are so telling and so remarkable. He comes into situations and cultures with the empathy of an insider, but the objectivity of an outsider. And it is clear he sees situations truly – objectively, as they are. "Truly, truly" are his commonest words ... and his teaching stands the test of time and history.

And yet he was criticised all through his ministry. The sum total of the criticisms is to confirm the bias of those criticising him! He is a threat because in Zygmunt Bauman's terms he is neither a complete insider (one of us), nor a complete outsider (one of them). This insight comes from Bauman's remarkable study, *Modernity and Ambivalence*, chapter 2. It is the study of the "stranger": one who is not to be categorised as either "friend" or "enemy". The crucifixion is a final comment on human inability to judge objectively or fairly.

PRAYERS

"Lord,
Sometimes I am aware of judging others. I suppose the truth is that more often I am blissfully unaware of my bias and selectivity. Is there any way out of this dilemma?"

"Child,

You are alive to the human dilemma and the lack of objectivity that prevents true listening and understanding. The most practical advice is to refrain from criticising others, and to leave judgement to me. And please don't forget to pray daily for forgiveness, especially when you feel you've had a pretty good run of being fair and consistent!"

5. Sinning

In the spring, at the time when kings go off to war, David sent Joab out with the king's men and the whole Israelite army. They destroyed the Ammonites, and besieged Rabbah. But David remained in Jerusalem.

One evening David got up from his bed and walked around on the roof of the palace. From the roof he saw a woman bathing. The woman was very beautiful, and David sent someone to find out about her. The man said, "Isn't this Bathsheba, the daughter of Eliam and the wife of Uriah the Hittite?" Then David sent messengers to get her. She came to him, and he slept with her. (She had purified herself from her uncleanness.) Then she went back home. The woman conceived and sent word to David saying, "I am pregnant."
2 SAMUEL 11:1-5

"Have mercy on me, O God,
 according to your unfailing love;
according to your great compassion
 blot out my transgressions.
Wash away all my iniquity
 and cleanse me from my sin.
For I know my transgressions,
 and my sin is always before me.
Against you, you only, have I sinned

and done what is evil in your sight,
   so that you are proved right when you speak
      and justified when you judge.
Surely I was sinful at birth,
      sinful from the time my mother conceived me.
Surely you desire truth in the inner parts,
      you teach me wisdom in the inmost place.
Cleanse me with hyssop, and I shall be clean;
      wash me and I shall be whiter than snow."

PSALM 51:1-7

THIS MEDITATION IS NOT about sex, any more than adultery is primarily about sex. In fact the most perfunctory reading of the story of David's sin (2 Samuel 11 and 12) uncovers the complexity and imbeddedness of his sin. At one level it is about a casual sexual act stimulated by a chance sighting of a beautiful woman, but it is so much more than this and the writer of this passage uses Jane Austen-like irony and analysis. David is inexplicably absent from the front-line during a war. David, the warrior-king who faced the Philistine giant alone, is now lazily whiling away his time while his soldiers are prepared to die for their country. A child is conceived as a result of sexual intercourse and this creates another element in the vicious circle. David tries to cover up his sin by subterfuge. He involves his commander; he withdraws Uriah from the front line for no military reason. Eventually he has Uriah murdered (there is no other more accurate term). He is overcome with remorse. Bathsheba is in mourning. The child dies. The word gets out so that Nathan hears about it. David's kingship and authority never recovers.

Sin does not, and cannot, exist in some form of splendid or sealed isolation. It must spread. Properly understood there is no such thing as a private sin, because life is not like that. Conscious and unconscious, personal and public, individual and collective: are all interwoven. Manifest effects can be hidden, but latent ones remain beneath the surface ready to emerge or erupt at unexpected times.

Psalm 51 is specifically related to David's sin and as such it is both moving and instructive. What David acknowledges is that this sin has affected and gathered up his whole personality and biography, and that it has offended God. He has seen into the heart of sin: it is about our nature, God's nature, and our relationship with him (as well as the more immediate and tangible human relationships). This means that dealing with it requires a complete "confession" with no holds barred; and a total cleansing. The psalm repays careful reading – not so much in the form of study or analysis, but at times when we are conscious of sin.

This brings us back to the question of sex and adultery. In a sexually "liberated" culture (21st century Western societies use this description of themselves) future historians will see an obsession with sexual matters. Setting aside such questions of definition, one of the effects is that issues other than those sexual tend to be seen in this light. Adultery is seen as a sexual indiscretion and treated comparatively lightly: if there is no resulting disease or pregnancy why all the fuss? What has happened is that the nature of marriage has been completely misunderstood. Adultery cannot be reduced simply to a sexual act or acts. It is something which involves two whole persons. It is a break of trust, of loyalty, of publicly-given and solemn oath. It is as serious and personal a social act as can be conceived. If we cannot trust a considered and public pledge before family, friends and community, what basis is there for any trust, or social life?

The story of David is as telling a treatise on this theme as it is possible to conceive, and Nathan the prophet makes no bones about his condemnation. Today we need a similar element of the prophetic; not a witch-hunt against individual or pet hates, but a dispassionate statement of the truth about the nature of sin.

Now this line of thought can seem so enfolding and complete that it becomes thoroughly depressing. Why go on? Because until the truth is recognised individuals and groups will suffer unease, depression, fear, suspicion and be unable to address them or deal with them. It is only when the root of sin and the source of its effects are acknowledged that we get beyond the salacious desire to describe and criticise, and down to the real business of healing and forgiveness. (For those able to lay their hands on them the T.S. Eliot plays *The Cocktail Party* and *The Family Reunion* are studies of this theme).

Perhaps the greatest irony of contemporary times is that so-called "sexual liberation" should be accompanied by such deep personal and collective unhappiness. To understand why, we need to understand the nature of society and the nature of sin. What seems depressing is actually releasing and liberating. We know the truth and it sets us free. Our faith centres on the truth that forgiveness of sin and healing of relationships are not only possible, but have begun, in Jesus.

PRAYERS

"Lord,
This whole reflection makes me aware of the splits in my life
between mind and heart; the attempted separation of personal
and social. But if I really started to be open about sin and
motives, where on earth will it end? Couldn't it result in
endless introspection?"

"Child
Your contemporary world is lost in endless collective
introspection. A recognition of the nature of sin is the only way
back to integrity, to joy and to my heart. Please understand
that the purpose of my commandments is to increase health
and happiness, and that the desire of my heart is that once sin
is confessed we might celebrate. Why don't you check out the
ending of the parables? What a spell has been cast! To think
that salvation is seen as anything less than freedom, and
forgiveness than joy!"

6. Deserting

The word of the LORD came to me: "Son of man, prophesy against the shepherds of Israel; prophesy and say to them: 'This is what the Sovereign LORD says: Woe to the shepherds of Israel who only take care of themselves! Should not shepherds take care of the flock? You eat the curds, clothe yourselves with the wool and slaughter the choice animals, but you do not take care of the flock. You have not strengthened the weak or healed the sick or bound up the injured. You have not brought back the strays or searched for the lost. You have ruled them harshly and brutally. So they were scattered because there was no shepherd, and when they were scattered they became food for all the wild animals. My sheep wandered over all the mountains and on every high hill. They were scattered over the whole earth, and no-one searched or looked for them.'"

EZEKIEL 34:1-6

With him was a crowd armed with swords and clubs, sent from the chief priests, the teachers of the law, and the elders.

Now the betrayer had arranged a signal with them: "The one I kiss is the man; arrest him and lead him away under guard." Going at once to Jesus, Judas said, "Rabbi!" and kissed him. The men seized Jesus and arrested him. Then one of those standing near drew his sword and struck the servant of the high priest, cutting off his ear.

"Am I leading a rebellion," said Jesus, "that you have come out with swords and clubs to capture me? Every day I was with you, teaching in the temple courts, and you did not arrest me. But the Scriptures must be fulfilled." Then everyone deserted him and fled.

MARK 14:43-50

A SHEPHERD DESERTING his flock inevitably consigns the whole herd to suffering and likely death. The shepherd is all that stands between each sheep and the very real wild animals of the Middle East, or the metaphorical wild animals of hunger, thirst and disease. No wonder Ezekiel, like other prophets, condemns such desertion unreservedly. Zechariah put it succinctly:

"Woe to the worthless shepherd,
who deserts the flock!
May the sword strike his arm and his right eye!
May his arm be completely withered,
his right eye totally blinded."
ZECHARIAH 11:17

Is the sin of the disciples really so extreme?

It's worth pondering their desertion with this thought in mind. Jesus has called the Twelve and for three years they have shared his every thought and action. At the heart of his life and teaching is the promise that he is a good shepherd who is ready, if necessary, to lay down his life for his sheep. He has reached the point where his whole mission and life are at stake. He asks for his disciples' support in Gethsemane in a particular form: "Watch with me". When a crowd arrives to arrest him, guided by Judas, his disciples desert him and flee for their lives. John Mark may have lingered a bit and was nearly caught, but the rest showed a clean pair of heels. They knew they were deserting him to save their own lives. Later they would be willing to die for him, as some almost certainly did, but for now their basic instinct for self-preservation overrides everything else. The remorse felt at this desertion is most fully expressed by Peter when, remembering his promise never to desert, he broke down and wept! Except in cases of extreme callousness or cynicism, remorse eventually catches up with deserters.

As Christians we sadly find ourselves, individually and collectively, deserting our Lord, in less dramatic but no less significant ways. At times of pressure and confrontation we take the easy option (the church has often done this as an institution). Those of us in pastoral or leadership positions are sometimes guilty of deserting the flock entrusted to us. All too often in marriage and families, vows and loyalties are broken and betrayed and the vulnerable are put at risk.

The other graphic depiction of desertion is, of course, that of the soldier. It is particularly relevant to us as Christians for when we begin to follow Jesus do we not promise to obey our leader, to serve him as our Lord, to fight and not to heed the cost? Some would no doubt water down the nature of our commitment, but undoubtedly the New Testament pictures a Christian relationship with Jesus as that between servant and Lord. To disobey can hardly be called anything less than desertion in such circumstances.

The picture of the shepherd goes even deeper than that of the soldier and servant, and is laden with biblical allusions, not least the threefold command of Jesus to Peter to "feed my sheep" (John 21). Enlisted in the service of Jesus, we are entrusted with the welfare of others. To be seen by him as shepherds is one of the highest honours that can be given to us.

The desertion of marriage partners and children can be wrapped up in less stark terms, but once again our vows are set in the context of his love and sacrifice. For example, "Husbands love your wives just as Christ loved the church and gave himself up for her" (Ephesians 5:25). To break such vows is a grave betrayal. No wonder there is so much remorse.

And there are, of course, those many other ways in which we desert our Lord and Master, our calling and his Kingdom. Others may be unconscious of our desertion but, like Peter, we know he knows! Like Peter we need to confess our desertion, to experience that gentle, sensitive but probing forgiveness of Jesus. Yet again we may be tempted to feel that everyone's welfare would be better served by playing down the seriousness of the sin, but yet again this is adequate neither in relation to the remorse felt, nor the nature of our relationship with Jesus.

This is where our meditation brings us: out of his infinite love Jesus our Lord has refused to desert us, even to the point of sacrificing his own life. He is the shepherd who has given his life for his sheep. That is the ultimate and underlying context of our life and relationships. If we play down the significance of our misdemeanours we indirectly begin to scale down the nature of his love for us. So let us call a spade a spade – we are deserters, who have betrayed our Lord and Saviour who gave his all for us. But the greater truth is that our Lord is slow to anger and abounding in steadfast love. He seems to rejoice more in the return of deserters than anything else. The homecoming, though painful, involves a welcome into his open arms.

PRAYERS

"Lord,
Is it a temptation or is it a genuine concern when I suggest that this whole line of thought is a bit heavy? Just think of the effect on those who are really low already! The last thing they need is more cause for remorse. For some reason I'm uneasy about the whole thing, though it has to be said that in my own case it rings uncannily true...."

"Child,
When Jesus was talking to Peter, that most famous of deserters, he was careful to address his words and counsel individually. Of course, that must be so, but to answer your question – your genuine concern is likely to become a temptation before long. You know, I know when you have deserted me ... let's be real about it so our reconciliation and celebration can be equally real!"

7. Misunderstanding

The vision concerning Judah and Jerusalem that Isaiah son of Amoz saw during the reigns of Uzziah, Ahaz and Hezekiah, kings of Judah.

Hear, O heavens! Listen, O earth!
*   For the LORD has spoken:*
"I reared children and brought them up,
*   but they have rebelled against me.*
The ox knows his master,
*   the donkey his owner's manger,*
but Israel does not know,
*   my people do not understand."*

ISAIAH 1:1-3

Then James and John, the sons of Zebedee, came to him. "Teacher," they said, we want you to do for us whatever we ask."

"What do you want me to do for you?" he asked.

They replied, "Let one of us sit at your right and the other at your left in your glory."

"You don't know what you are asking," Jesus said. "Can you drink the cup I drink or be baptised with the baptism I am baptised with?"

"We can," they answered.

> *Jesus said to them, "You will drink the cup I drink and be baptised with the baptism I am baptised with, but to sit at my right or left is not for me to grant. These places belong to those for whom they have been prepared."*
> MARK 10:35-40

SOMETIMES PEOPLE GO ASTRAY, not because they deliberately choose to, but because of a misunderstanding. A little difference of opinion over what was meant can lead to a big difference of position over time and distance! The gap between God's intentions and the understanding of the people of Israel portrayed by Isaiah, was massive. There seemed to be virtually no insight into what God meant. It could be said to be one of the themes of the book. "Stop bringing meaningless offerings!" (Isaiah 1:13). The people see and hear but do not understand: God's thoughts are not their thoughts. It will only be when God's kingdom is established that "the eyes of those who see will no longer be closed, and the ears of those who hear will listen. The mind of the rash will know and understand, and the stammering tongue will be fluent and clear." (Isaiah 32:3-4).

In church history we see misunderstandings of other traditions and eras clearly. Sometimes it is God's nature that is misunderstood: sometimes the teaching of Scripture: sometimes the leadership of the church: sometimes his will for his world, and worship. A list seems tantalisingly and depressingly long. Were there periods without misunderstanding? It might be that we are incapable fully of interpreting God's intentions individually and collectively for more than flashes of insight and transitory periods of commitment.

The best test of this could be in the relationship between Jesus and his disciples. The Twelve surely had a chance to understand God's nature and intentions: after all, they ate, walked and talked with Jesus for three years continuously. Obviously they took much of his meaning on board but their misunderstanding is chronic. The kingdom of God is one of Jesus' central concerns: he taught about it frequently and with great care and ingenuity. Yet James and John missed the point completely and even after his death and resurrection the group still look for a restoration of the kingdom to Israel (Acts 1: 6). To take a charitable view we could say that the message was so radical that even after 2000 years most committed Christians still miss the point.

The degree of misunderstanding that exists in the world is often underestimated. Even in the counselling dyad, one to one, a skilled therapist knows only too well how difficult it is to hear what the client is saying, without imposing on it personal desire or memory and categories. How often in families, nuclear and extended, mistrust and even violence have grown up and lasted for generations because there was no real shared understanding of a particular action or event. This same process is at work in communities, organisations, nations as well as between them. People may have fundamental disagreements but there is possibly more agreement than we understood.

The human condition is such that we cannot see into another's heart, mind and will in any direct or pure sense. Pondering this at length one realises the difficulty of any meaningful communication. Philosophers are aware of levels of meaning and categories of thought; the psychiatrist conscious of unconscious motivations and transference; the anthropologist reflects on the completely different meanings attached to rituals from one culture to another; the theologian seeks convincing hermeneutic processes or principles. If we really knew how little we understood we might be shocked at our predicament!

But this awareness leads us on to the discovery of the lifelong art of listening, of empathy, of real conversation and reciprocity. We begin to sense the power of Buber's *I and Thou* where the other is allowed to become an authentic person in his or her own right and not just an instrument of ours or someone else. We see why Jane Austen and others attached so much importance to imagination as a way of bridging huge personal and intellectual gulfs. We begin to take in the relevance and insight of the one who pleaded: "I beseech you in the bowels of Christ, consider you may be mistaken".

The ability of Jesus to understand what was going on (not least the misunderstanding of others!) is both a comfort and a challenge. He did so because his own agenda and personality did not come between him and another. It is also significant that his parting gift to the church was the Holy Spirit who "will guide you into all truth" (or we might say "help you to navigate through all problems of misunderstanding"). The spirit in this respect is not about seeing something extra, divine, transcendent, but the means of seeing things as they are, pure and simple. The process may include moments of insight and disclosure but the art of avoiding misunderstanding is a lifelong one that has taxed the greatest of minds and saints.

PRAYERS

"Lord,
I've often thought the disciples were rather dense given the nearness and accessibility of Jesus. Now I begin to wonder whether they weren't more normal than that! I know how often people misunderstand what I mean and intend, so it's likely that I'm having difficulty too. But is there a way through?"

"Child,
The moment you ask that question you are on the threshold of finding the way. Misunderstandings all start with taken-for-granted assumptions and prejudices, and they can only be dispelled by the light of questioning and truth. My Spirit is sometimes confused with certainty. It's much more subtle than that – questions rather than answers, searching rather than finding, listening rather than teaching. Possibly my Spirit is more misunderstood than anything else ... but we've done enough for one day together. I think we're understanding one another just now ...."

8. Declining

Now the Israelites went out to fight against the Philistines. The Israelites camped at Ebenezer, and the Philistines at Aphek. The Philistines deployed their forces to meet Israel, and as the battle spread, Israel was defeated by the Philistines, who killed about four thousand of them on the battlefield. When the soldiers returned to camp, the elders of Israel asked, "Why did the LORD bring defeat upon us today before the Philistines? Let us bring the ark of the LORD's covenant from Shiloh, so that it may go with us and save us from the hand of our enemies."
I SAMUEL 4:1-3

"To the angel of the church in Ephesus write:
These are the words of him who holds the seven stars in his right hand and walks among the seven golden lampstands: I know your deeds, your hard work and your perseverance. I know that you cannot tolerate wicked men, that you have tested those who claim to be apostles but are not, and have found them false. You have persevered and have endured hardships for my name, and have not grown weary.
Yet I hold this against you: You have forsaken your first love. Remember the height from which you have fallen! Repent and do the things you did at first. If you do not repent, I will come to you and remove your lampstand from its place."
REVELATION 2:1-5

IN A SENSE DECLINE is part of the natural order. We talk of people declining as they get older and each day the sun declines as it sets. This is not the end but the end of a life or a day: the resurrection of the body, the new day, are not far away. It is perfectly normal too for organisations and nations to grow old and to give way, give birth to new ones. However, we accept the dignity of those who recognise declining faculties and resources but remain true to their faith and calling.

The type of decline described in 1 Samuel is something far more sad and serious. Essentially the moral rot in Israel, typified in the priestly family of Eli, has now affected everything. (It is like *Hamlet*'s Denmark.) Samuel as a boy was called (unforgettably) by God to reveal to Eli the seriousness of the situation: Eli's sons had sinned and he had not restrained them (1 Samuel 3:13). In time the nation itself became so weak it was defeated by the Philistines. The awful desolation of the defeated people is summed up in the name Eli's daughter-in-law gave to her son: Ichabod – "The glory of the Lord has departed from Israel".

A similar decline takes place in the life of King David at the time of Absalom's rebellion (2 Samuel 15:1-19:8). His sense of guilt, remorse and failure spreads through the nation. In his case the decline is halted but the zest, vigour, faith, trust of his former years never returns – the glory of the Lord has departed from him too.

The letter to the Ephesians compares the declining relationship between this church and Jesus Christ to that of two lovers. In terms that are so very familiar the church is told that it has lost its first love. The warning comes to repent before estrangement sets in, one of the recurring themes of Scripture in the Old and New Testaments. The overflowing devotion and love the people show for God declines to the point where their covenant marriage is in danger of ending in divorce.

Relationships do change – the freshness, immediacy, excitement of the early encounters cannot continue forever. We associate this particularly with lovers, but Weber demonstrates that the "charismatic stage" of an organisation's life is transitory. A form of routinisation is inevitable – indeed is beneficial, given growth and the need for stability. The problems come when we either assume that because the nature of the relationship changes God has become lukewarm towards us, or that we don't notice the process and so make no adjustment.

Any alert and committed sportsman or sportswoman will adjust their technique over the years as the full suppleness or speed of reflexes decline. These can be compensated for by careful strategy and technique for a time. But then comes the need to let go and recognise that life is about more than sheer competitiveness in one specific field. In our walk with God there will be changes over the years but there is always that awareness that as the external, physical decline occurs, the inner fire of faith can grow. In the terms of C.S. Lewis' *The Great Divorce* we become more solid.

The body may stoop, the hearing and eyesight may dim but the decline not only does not affect the soul, it can be said that the soul continues to thrive and develop. Not long before he died Dr. Martyn Lloyd-Jones preached at the church where I was the minister. It was the occasion of the church anniversary. After the service he spoke to me in the vestry: "Was it all right?" "That's a strange question coming from so eminent a preacher as you," I replied. "I know," he continued wistfully, "but you see as I get older people are saying I simply don't know when to stop preaching. I'm inclined to ramble. The problem is that every day Jesus seems more wonderful and I want to say all I can about him in case it's my last chance!" I assured him that he had helped me to understand something more of the supreme beauty and loveliness of Christ.

Eli sadly did not have this inner fire: this close personal relationship with God that called him with irresistible force. For him and for Israel the decline was complete.

PRAYERS

"Lord,
How is that inner fire, faith and hope kept alive? You know how dead things can be, whether in a personal relationship, or in a church, at times. I sense it's not necessarily a question of

technique or even commitment, though I do see it involves the will as well as the emotions."

"Child,
Have you seen those married couples whose love is alive after thirty, forty, fifty years? Have you chatted with those followers of mine who are well advanced in years and the faith? There is a covenant or act of will, but the fire comes from the relationship. There is the spark of my Spirit, a dance between us that is forever growing more sensitive and beautiful. Not faster, or more complex, but more real. The decline of the outer shell reveals the truth about the soul. "

Part 5 LOOKING FORWARD

Growing   Learning

Exploring   Dreaming

Watching   Praying

Preparing   Hoping

A ND SO WE COME to the last of our five themes. It is time to look forward, not as an escape from the past or present, not as something separate from daily life, but in recognition of the expectation and hope that lies deep within the meantime. We have travelled together in this series of meditations through a range of moods and experiences. At times you may have wondered whether they were too cutting, too honest and too personal. They have been uneven and sometimes, perhaps, off-track. The section on going astray, in particular, seemed to offer little comfort seen in isolation. Why so? In part, because the purpose of this book is to seek to discover and face realities: to drive towards the nub or heart of an issue, and not to flinch from the truth and its implications. The meantime cannot hide such bedrock under a surface of spiritual highs or frenzied business and action. There is nowhere to hide. But there is a deeper reason implicit and written in all this. It is that we believe as an Easter people that we have every reason to look forward to the future with hope.

This is so much part of the Christian faith that in a very real way we take it for granted. We have imbibed the great truths of the scriptures and know that ultimately nothing will separate us from the love of God in Christ. The Day of the Lord will come. The Kingdom will be established. Every knee will bow before Jesus as he is acknowledged as Lord. There will be no more sorrow or crying. Death will not have the final say. Death itself will die and be swallowed up in victory. Though the universe will continue to wind down, there will be a new heaven and earth.

The Christian community is set within a framework of covenant hope. The rainbow promise endures for ever. There are trials, frustrations, setbacks, losses, betrayals, periods of wandering and misunderstanding. Daily life may seem and feel black, empty and uncharted but as we trust step by step there is the awareness that our Saviour and Lord has made footprints for us – that he is ahead. Those footprints are fresh and in them there is as it were evidence of his wounds. He is not here: he is risen.

There is a temptation to look to the next big event or promise to save or rescue us from our predicament in just the way a clinically depressed person can tend to place enormous expectations on the next meeting or conversation with a friend or counsellor. Churches can live for the next revelation of God's will, the next picture or prophecy. The anticipation of which this section speaks is rather that which makes sense of the meantime itself. It does not assume that the meantime will end this week, next week, or even in our life-time, but that what we see and experience as ordinary or even painful is part of a cosmic symphony, a universal revolution and rebirth, such that everything will one day be seen to have had its place. All shall be well and all manner of things shall be well.

1. Growing

Now Joseph and all his brothers and all that generation died, but the Israelites were fruitful and multiplied greatly and became exceedingly numerous, so that the land was filled with them.

Then a new king, who did not know about Joseph, came to power in Egypt. "Look," he said to his people, "the Israelites have become much too numerous for us. Come, we must deal shrewdly with them or they will become even more numerous and, if war breaks out, will join our enemies, fight against us and leave the country."

So they put slave masters over them to oppress them with forced labour, and they built Pithom and Rameses as store cities for Pharaoh. But the more they were oppressed, the more they multiplied and spread.
EXODUS 1:6-12

He told them another parable: "The kingdom of heaven is like a mustard seed, which a man took and planted in his field. Though it is the smallest of all your seeds, yet when it grows, it is the largest of garden plants and becomes a tree, so that the birds of the air come and perch in its branches."

He told them still another parable: "The kingdom of heaven is like yeast that a woman took and mixed into a large amount of flour until it worked all through the dough."
MATTHEW 13:31-33

I consider that our present sufferings are not worth comparing with the glory that will be revealed in us. The creation waits in eager expectation for the sons of God to be revealed. For the creation was subjected to frustration, not by its own choice, but by the will of the one who subjected it, in hope that the creation itself will be liberated from its bondage to decay and brought into the glorious freedom of the children of God.

We know that the whole creation has been groaning as in the pains of childbirth right up to the present time. Not only so, but we ourselves, who have the firstfruits of the Spirit, groan inwardly as we wait eagerly for our adoption as sons, the redemption of our bodies. For in this hope we were saved.

ROMANS 8:18-24

T HESE THREE PASSAGES are as representative of the whole sweep of scripture's meantime as any. The first focuses on the formative 430 years of Israel's history; the second on Christ's insight into the nature of kingdom of God. The passage from Romans is perhaps the greatest exposition of the Christian view of history. They have in common the theme of growth. In the case of the Israelites it is numerical growth; in the case of the two parables of the kingdom it is physical growth; in the case of history it is gestation leading to new birth and a new creation.

It is appropriate that two of the readings are wrapped in pain and suffering – they are no ordinary growing pains either! Growth is not something that happens only in pleasant times, or when pain has ceased. Growth takes place in and through suffering. How do we make sense of the meantimes of our lives, our families, of churches, of history? They are all part of a process that is quiet, often unnoticed, but irresistible. The two parables are disarmingly simple – rarely reflected upon as are, say, the parables of the Good Samaritan or the Prodigal Son, but they unlock deep insights into the meantime.

Because they are so obviously about "normal" or everyday life, as distinct from moments of great import or unusual manifestations, they help us to see that the kingdom of heaven (their subject) is about the everyday (as well as the special as exemplified by the pearl of great price or the discovered treasure). They do not exhaust our understanding of the kingdom but they are vital for any true understanding. In focusing on the meantime we may have stumbled on a pearl of great price! Put another way, if we centre our thought and action on special revelations or experiences we may miss out on the kingdom!

Both parables are about growth and implicitly call our attention to the need for time. Neither process can be cut short or sped up. Growth requires time. Time is perhaps one of the most vital ingredients. It is so obvious but therefore so easily missed. For the problem confronting many is the sheer amount of time spent in the meantime – the days, months and years roll on and there seems to be no answer to prayers and no resolution of tension, no shape to progress. We ask God how long we must wait for the Day of the Lord. But while this is going on he is granting us that most precious commodity – time.

When we are living alongside growing children their growth can be very difficult to notice. Others who see them less frequently often notice the change immediately: hence the common greeting when meeting a child after a year of two: "My, how you've grown!" In understanding the natural world we have become used to the technology that enables us to speed up film of a plant or animal so that the growth happens before our eyes. In fact it is before our eyes if we stay with it, but requires time and patience if we are not to miss it. Growth involves a deep understanding of the nature of time as it intersects our lives.

Both the growth of the mustard seed and the yeast in the dough are marked by their quietness. There is no sound at all. Jesus could have drawn attention to a growing child or animal, but he did not. The mustard seed and the yeast do not attract notice and certainly would create no headlines in the media. And this is so significant in understanding the meantime and the kingdom: those looking for labels, admission fees, drum-rolls and heightened experiences are likely to miss out.

But both processes come to a climax after however long it takes. The mustard seed eventually provides shelter for the bird; the yeast affects the whole dough causing it to rise, ready for baking. There is an "until" in both stories – not involving something dramatic, but providing a sense of completion. Growing does not go on forever, endlessly, shapelessly, limitlessly. And so it is with the kingdom – the "until" is a quiet word of hope, bringing with it echoes of the last supper: "... proclaim the Lord's death until he comes" (1 Corinthians 11:26).

Nothing is completely static on earth – it is either dying or growing, however slowly and imperceptibly. The Kingdom of Heaven is growing and those who seek it need the eyes of faith, patience and hope. There is no promise of the time scale. But neither the process nor the fact that there will be a conclusion are in doubt.

PRAYERS

"Lord,
There is something about the position of the observer in all this too, isn't there? What seems like death to a particular person or group may be revealed to others at another time or place as a birth following a long period of gestation. It's almost as if the person or group growing are the least likely to know about it!"

"Child,
That's a beautiful thought. If it were possible for you to be everywhere and at the same time anticipating, experiencing, and recollecting a process you would see how obvious it all is, and how wonderful. Because humans can't, they are pathologically inclined to seek sense, salvation or meaning in superficial and glossy "events". The real wonder, the real truth which we will one day share, is about the whole, not any particular part. You will see it all when you stand where I stand and sit where I sit. In the meantime let this hope not draw you away from the every day but into it with a fresh sense of wonder and awe."

2. Learning

Now Moses was tending the flock of Jethro his father-in-law, the priest of Midian, and he led the flock to the far side of the desert and came to Horeb, the mountain of God.
EXODUS 3:1

Now David was the son of an Ephrathite named Jesse, who was from Bethlehem in Judah. Jesse had eight sons, and in Saul's time he was old and well advanced in years. Jesse's three oldest sons had followed Saul to the war: The firstborn was Eliab, the second, Abinadab; and the third, Shammah. David was the youngest. The three oldest followed Saul, but David went back and forth from Saul to tend his father's sheep at Bethlehem.
I SAMUEL 17:12-15

THESE PASSAGES DESCRIBE two of the most perfect learning experiences in history, though it might not have seemed so at the time. Moses had murdered an Egyptian and fled to the desert of Midian, fearing presumably that this would be how he would see out the rest of his life. He was forty at the time of the murder and he was in Midian until he was eighty! It could hardly have seemed less relevant to anything he might ever do in retirement (should his life sentence ever end) for his own people were in civilised Egypt and to rescue them was as impossible as rejoining them.

In fact these years were God's learning experience for Moses. He was with a very wise father-in-law from whom he no doubt learned much of the received non-Egyptian wisdom of the time. He learned the trade of shepherd, which is about leadership, caring and patience. He learned about ordinary family life outside the palace. And everything there was to know about the desert, day and night, summer and winter, rivers and plains, mountains and oases, plants and animals. Put together, this was the place where he would lead the people of Israel for another forty years until he was one hundred and twenty! It was like forty years of a tailor-made university course for his precise role.

There are echoes of the time of Moses in David's. Overshadowing David's age was the Philistine threat to his people. His brothers, obviously soldiers, were virtually helpless in the face of the Philistines, who had all the modern weaponry. So of what relevance was David's experience as a shepherd? It was to be the basis of every stage of his life, teaching him principles of leadership, acquainting him with the intricacies of the geography of much of the land, not least how to sleep rough which was so necessary when on the run from Saul. It provided him with the opportunities to contemplate God's natural world and to learn to play the harp (not only in the Psalms so wonderfully used, but also in Saul's court). And not least it trained him in the very art (sling throwing) that was to lead to the most famous defeat of the Philistines. When convincing Saul that he can take on Goliath he has the necessary skills and also a trust in God that sees everything coming together. He is quietly confident.

Throughout Scripture we see how God has ways of providing learning experiences we would never have considered. Jesus is thirty years in Nazareth? Paul – years of rabbinical study and experience in persecuting Christians? Peter – a fisherman? And nations and peoples also have unexpected and unusual learning experiences – forty years in a desert; generations dispersed in Babylon of all places!

Seeing that this is so common in Scripture may give us just a little more confidence in our own lives. It is precisely those times, when we are experiencing the ordinariness of life to such an extent that it is like a wilderness experience or a dark night of the soul, that we may be learning most for future roles and service. How often suffering, trauma, bereavement, provides the soil in which future ministries and insights thrive. I have seen this so frequently in others but in my own experience it has been equally true.

The three degrees I took have been a rich mine of resources for lecturing, writing, administering. But the time as a social worker in West Pilton, Edinburgh was, as my students know, a period when I learned once and for all what poverty was, what it meant to be marginalised and oppressed, how inequalities could exist so close to each other without ever engaging. I can see that now. But in fact I had taken the job because my research funding had come to an end. I had to do something! It was a traumatic period for all sorts of reasons and came to an abrupt end. But how I thank God for this experience of a council housing estate and the families I still remember by name and admire.

If we really believe God is sovereign (and this has staggering implications for us as individuals as well as a church and nation) then we can rest assured that there is no experience he cannot turn into a learning experience, a source of inspiration, wisdom and insight. Only today I had a letter from a relative in South Africa. She has lost her only son and her grandchild in motor accidents. Her grandchild was in the car she was driving. She told how she had become angry, shaken, numb, bewildered to the core but how she had become in touch with the core in such a way that there was now no situation she could not face in the name of Jesus, and a world of suffering where she understood, often without words, what the sufferers felt.

The meantime is a learning period, and the full purpose of the lessons is never fully apparent in the present.

"Lord,
I see all this so clearly but it's such an act of faith when you're actually in the wilderness. Later on you can begin to trace the pathway and make some sense of things, but not when you're in it. Help me to trust you and to encourage that trust in others."

"Child,
There is no way to my heart, or to the heart of others, without the wilderness, and yet by its very nature it cannot be understood except by faith. Most are experiencing something of that learning process most of the time. It's the most significant aspect of the meantime for all who seek to serve me. The names differ: wilderness, rejection, Gethsemane, they always refer to the time or place where the learning experience is most concentrated and real."

3. Exploring

The LORD said to Moses, "Send some men to explore the land of Canaan, which I am giving to the Israelites. From each ancestral tribe send one of its leaders." So at the LORD's command Moses sent them out from the Desert of Paran. All of them were leaders of the Israelites.
NUMBERS 13:1-3

As the men started on their way to map out the land, Joshua instructed them, "Go and make a survey of the land and write a description of it. Then return to me, and I will cast lots for you here at Shiloh in the presence of the LORD." So the men left and went through the land. They wrote its description on a scroll, town by town, in seven parts, and returned to Joshua in the camp at Shiloh. Joshua then cast lots for them in Shiloh in the presence of the LORD, and there he distributed the land to the Israelites according to their tribal divisions.
JOSHUA 18:8-10

"I pray that out of his glorious riches he may strengthen you with power through his Spirit in your inner being, so that Christ may dwell in your hearts through faith. And I pray that you, being rooted and established in love, may have power, together with all the saints, to grasp how wide and long and high and deep is the love of Christ, and to know this love

that surpasses knowledge – that you may be filled to the measure of all the fullness of God."
EPHESIANS 3:16-19

THE SPIES WERE SENT OUT to explore Canaan soon after the Israelites had been led out of Egypt. It may seem an exciting (and therefore "non-meantime" event) but it was routine. A nomadic people could not begin to invade and settle in a land without first exploring it, and before settlement was possible there had to be some careful mapping (Joshua 18). The exploration is reported to have taken forty days – that special biblical period of time with so many associations. It is the period of the wilderness, the meantime, the ordinary – not the moment or day of vision or conquest.

The echo is particularly loud in this case because it was the people's reaction to the majority report of the spies that resulted in the forty years wilderness experience of the Israelites (Numbers 14). That exploration was purposeful and exclusive. It was to examine every conceivable practical aspect of Canaan in the light of the promised entry to possess the land. Exploration is a process set in the context of some future purpose or plan. There may be those who are, as it were, professional explorers, but they are resourced by others who have long-term goals and aspirations.

Apart from the great moments of discovery in history (those of Columbus, Vasco da Gama and Captain Cook, for example) we tend to know little, but the process took centuries and the most common experience was not great new worlds found and reported, but failure, loss and death. And this geographical exploration can serve as a symbol of the explorations of science, medicine, psychology and theology. As a species, humans are created with that desire, or instinct, to explore. The young toddler is so obviously bent on exploration and the word "why?" forms a substantial part of the usual vocabulary of every young child. The state of exploration in human history at this point in time is more exciting than ever before: the smallest elements of energy, the farthest galaxies, the recesses of the mind and intricacies of genetics. No wonder T.S. Eliot ended his *Four Quartets* on this very theme:

> *"We shall not cease from exploration ..."*
> *We can do no other.*

This is as true of the spiritual dimension of life as any other and the passage from Ephesians, set within a context of a description of Christ that is as grand and awe-inspiring as any in the New Testament (chapter 1), is an encouragement to explore the spiritual riches of Christ. The process is one that will not end but will involve every aspect of life and experience – our inner being, our heart, faith, love and knowledge. What is more it is a process of opening ourselves up to one who longs to reveal more than we can ever ask or think. It is not a one way exploration, but mutual exploration and revelation.

Though many do explore and though the instinct for exploration is so powerful, it is still a minority pursuit. Most settle for the routine of the known paths. The Israelites, like all prisoners, found a security in the rigid and predictable confines of slavery, and all through history we have resisted radical exploration of mind as well as body, preferring "self-perpetuating belief systems" to the challenges of the frontiers and beyond.

We are called as Christians to be explorers, seekers, followers of the way, those fixing our eyes on Jesus the pioneer of our faith. There are those who have experienced great spiritual discoveries (Abraham, Moses, Isaiah, Paul, in Biblical times, and a host of others since then, male and female, throughout the world), but for most of us it is a quiet process of waiting and reflection. We see a relationship, a person, in a new light. We come to the place in scripture again and understand something more; we find ourselves in changing situations and have to work out our bearings afresh. The meantime of exploration, as in research, is largely routine and unexceptional. We explore not because we will make a great discovery, but because we are made that way.

Our family community has a base in North Wales and we spend weeks each summer there enjoying the richly varied mountains, rivers, beaches and bays. No holiday is complete without what we call our "expedition". It involves two or three days in the hills with overnight camping near a llyn (lake) at 1,500 feet or above. On one occasion in the Rhinog Hills one of the family asked if he could do some climbing before breakfast. On his return he was alive with excitement. Pointing at the rugged, heather-covered crags to the west of the tents and across the llyn he exclaimed, "It's brilliant. It's like one big adventure playground."

> "Lord,
> Is there any antidote for getting caught up in self-perpetuating belief systems? They seem to trap all but the most daring explorers, especially Christians and those committed to other faiths. I don't mean I'm a Pascal or Einstein or Bonhoeffer or Luther, or Thomas á Kempis or Julian of Norwich ...."

> "Child,
> Follow me ... I'm never to be found at exactly the last place where you met me. As they said of Jesus: 'He is not here. He is risen and gone before you.'"

4. Dreaming

*In the twenty-fifth year of our exile, at the beginning of the year, on the
tenth of the month, in the fourteenth year after the fall of the city – on
that very day the hand of the LORD was upon me and he took me there.
In visions of God he took me to the land of Israel and set me on a very
high mountain, on whose south side were some buildings that looked like
a city. He took me there, and I saw a man whose appearance was like
bronze; he was standing in the gateway with a linen cord and a
measuring rod in his hand. The man said to me, "Son of man, look with
your eyes and hear with your ears and pay attention to everything I am
going to show you, for that is why you have been brought here. Tell the
house of Israel everything you see."*

EZEKIEL 40:1-4

*Then I saw a new heaven and a new earth, for the first heaven and the
first earth had passed away, and there was no longer any sea. I saw the
Holy City, the new Jerusalem, coming down out of heaven from God,
prepared as a bride beautifully dressed for her husband. And I heard a
loud voice from the throne saying, "Now the dwelling of God is with men,
and he will live with them. They will be his people, and God himself will
be with them and be their God. He will wipe every tear from their eyes.*

There will be no more death or mourning or crying or pain, for the old order of things has passed away."
REVELATION 21:1-4

THE PLACE OF DREAMS and visions in Scripture is often underestimated. Dreams are one of God's common ways of revealing the truth, his will, to human beings. Likewise dreams are a major means of entering into another person's world, hence the studies by the psychiatrists Freud and Jung, the Freudians and the Jungians.

There are special visions dated in place and time that transform a person's life and become a focus of attention. The vision of Isaiah comes into this category (Isaiah 6). But by definition this is not the ordinary or meantime – you do not date eras by the dreams of the everyday. The point here is that in periods of wilderness, of isolation, of barrenness some of the most far-reaching and beautiful insights into the true nature of things have come.

One of the most moving and influential speeches of the twentieth century was that by Martin Luther King: "I Have a Dream." It was produced during a period when overt slavery had given way to the more subtle oppression of black people – decades of longing for true freedom and respect. It has the power to move years later for it peers into a future age when relationships between men and women, black and white, old and young, rich and poor, will be characterised by respect and trust and the absence of fear. Generations of people each living in the meantime look forward to a new era, a new dawn, and this speech encapsulates an understanding of the ordinary in the new age.

Ezekiel has his dreams or visions in the exile, a period of Jewish history. The Temple has been destroyed and Jerusalem burnt to the ground, many of the people are slaves in Babylon. Yet Ezekiel sees a most detailed picture of what is to be. A new temple, measured in every respect, is described. At first it seems clinical, almost lifeless, but then the glory of the Lord is revealed. "His voice was like the roar of rushing waters, and the land was radiant with his glory" (Ezekiel 43:2). The Temple is at the centre of a city and the city is at the centre of a nation and the name of the city is "The Lord is There".

John is exiled on the island of Patmos writing the Book of Revelation which culminates in a series of visions of the New Jerusalem. In a way remarkably described by Austin Farrer in *The Glass of Vision*, John recreates from the vision of Ezekiel a new vision. The Temple becomes the City, and the land of Israel has become the world. All time and history come together in a new creation. The end of the dispensation is portrayed: the end of the meantime will come. Many have wanted to delve into the nature of the future creation drawing on sources way beyond Ezekiel and Revelation to make their points. But that is not our purpose here. There will be an end to the meantime for all. The new creation will beggar description as the dream becomes a reality.

But what of the meantime and its relationship to the visions? The visions gather up collective memories of past glories and present time in a new way. The past has not been lost forever. Defeat is not final. They are to provide a contrast with the present and the visions are exactly what is not happening in any visible way. They provide hope that one day, however far removed in the future, things will be different. There is an end to the slavery, to the nightmare. So they gather together past, present and future. If however that were all, it would be to talk of the visions as an escape – something separate from, other than, the here and now.

This is where the true relationship between the dream and the everyday can be seen. They are not just visions of the future but also a description of the heart of things, how things are, the Kingdom of Heaven now, as well as then. The meaning is attached to the opening of the revelation of John: "Write, therefore, what you have seen, what is now and what will take place later", in that what follows describes the now and the future. Ezekiel, like John, is far from home: at the will of others. Yet the message is for now. It is to be told now. Why? Not just to give encouragement and hope, but to reveal the true nature of the present.

For the truth is that this vision of God's glory, of his spirit, of his presence is a present reality. Seen with the eyes of faith the meantime is not a wilderness at heart. It is a reality centred on the Sovereign Lord.

What seemed like tragedy is not so in ultimate terms. The beyond is in the midst. The Eternal is now. It may be that you read this in a prison cell, a hospital bed, a shanty town, a wilderness – if so you are no farther away from the glory of God's presence than Ezekiel or John. You may long for a future different from today, but that should not blind you to the presence of God in the midst.

It's the sort of experience described in 2 Kings 6:15-17, which is a good place to end this meditation, for the dream is seen to be true.

PRAYERS

"Lord,
Some churches seem to be full of people dreaming dreams,
seeing pictures and having visions. So often they imply the
meantime should be over by next week, by your intervention,
by our efforts, and a mini-Pentecost occurring very soon. I'm
not sure what to do about them (and those who attach so
much significance to them)."

"Child,
These are all fragments of the visions and dreams of which Joel
spoke. There is a cosmic renewal going on – the spell of Babel
has been broken. My kingdom is real, though not yet complete.
One day you will see it. But do not mistake a part for the whole
and do not let anything draw attention from the true glory of
the here and now, deep at the heart of things. What is set in the
future, as a concrete reality, is also now in a fuller way."

5. Watching

"Son of man, I have made you a watchman for the house of Israel; so hear the word I speak and give them warning from me. When I say to the wicked, 'O wicked man, you will surely die,' and you do not speak out to dissuade him from his ways, that wicked man will die for his sin, and I will hold you accountable for his blood. But if you do warn the wicked man to turn from his ways and he does not do so, he will die for his sin, but you will be saved yourself."
EZEKIEL 33:7-9

"No-one knows about the day or hour, not even the angels in heaven, nor the Son, but only the Father. Be on guard! Be alert! You do not know when that time will come. It's like a man going away: he leaves his house and puts his servants in charge, each with his assigned task, and tells the one at the door to keep watch.

"Therefore keep watch because you do not know when the owner of the house will come back – whether in the evening, or at midnight, or when the cock crows, or at dawn. If he comes suddenly, do not let him find you sleeping. What I say to you, I say to everyone: 'Watch!'"
MARK 13:32-37

Unless the LORD watches over the city,
the watchmen stand guard in vain.
PSALM 127:1

THE WORDS OF PSALM 127 still adorn the old watchman's house in Ripon, at the south-west corner of the market place. They are a link with the time when cities were small, compact and fortified with walls. Each night the gates (east gate, north gate etc.) would be locked and the task of the watchman was to ensure the safety of the city both internally and externally.

The watchman is therefore a fine symbol of the role of the prophet: always alert for signs of unrest or injustice within the community of faith and also for messengers or armies from without. The watchman's only equipment, apart from his eyesight, was a trumpet, which was blown to warn the city's inhabitants of the arrival of visitors, friendly or menacing. The role has particular poignancy in Ezekiel's case because of the impending disaster to fall upon Jerusalem. "The city is fallen" is the message that arrives in verse 21 of Ezekiel 33.

The image spills over into the role of the shepherd as watching is one of his key tasks so "the watchmen" and "the shepherd" are symbols for leadership of the Jewish community. Thus Jesus urges his followers to watch and pray. The Day of the Lord will come but the timing is unknown. The attitude of Christians should therefore be one of alertness as distinct from drowsiness or laziness.

The vital hours of the watch are at night. No-one who has ever had responsibility for being on guard during the night will ever forget some of the associations: the stillness, the freshness of the air, the night sky, the birdsong, the streaks of grey and the crimson as the dawn begins to break. Some years ago on a mountaineering expedition I had to attend to the pressing needs of one of our party in the early hours. I gave the person my sleeping bag and then had to spend the rest of the night keeping warm. It was on the slopes of the Glyders in Gwynedd, and the experience of waiting for the dawn as I wandered around the slopes of Idwal in the cold night air was quite different from any other on numerous trips.

The Christian awaits the dawn which marks the glorious end of the meantime for ever. Paul puts this dramatically towards the end of Romans (13:11-12). And we shall return to this thought in a while. But there is another vital task in the meantime: we are to be alert to what is going on within our communities and societies. A well-known British Bible college has talked of Christians having the Bible in one hand and the newspaper in the other. The point is a fair one (despite the fact that it rather over-emphasises the place of reading in everyday life!). Those who rely on one or the other miss out on a vital interplay between the two. The Bible challenges our fashions and assumptions as children of our culture and time; the newspaper challenges our understanding of the Bible.

The church is to be a watchman in society, and if it is not then it has misunderstood one of its primary tasks. It may not be able to enforce its call to action, but it is a dereliction of duty not to be alert and to warn. A good title for church reports is "a call to church and nation": that is the watchman's job in a nutshell.

Once again we see that it is in the lonely night hours when everyone else slumbers and should be sleeping that we understand the significance of our own roles and tasks in the meantime. And we can keep alert because the meantime has an end: if it didn't the role of watchman would become impossible. As we look ahead we have intimations of the new day and era that will dawn.

In 1969 I was on a boat approaching Israel. As dawn broke over Carmel the Israelis on board broke into song. We sailed into Haifa with those songs accompanying the first rays of sunlight. It was not just another harbour and stop, but in some sense, for them the harbour and the dawn. Isaiah evokes this same sense when writing: (Isaiah 52:7-10). And this great prophecy had in its time inspired many fellow travellers. We must not speculate on the nature and timing of the dawn but, in the sure and certain knowledge that it will come, we must accept the ancient and noble mantle of watchman.

"Lord,
One of the great differences between the time when watchmen held sway and now is that very few people seem to take notice of warnings issued in your name. In the defence of the majority it has to be said that often the trumpet has a rather uncertain sound!"

"Child,
There is no prophet or watchman of mine who has not experienced the loneliness of seeing the gravity or potential joy of a situation and finding others unable to respond. But I sense your focus is on big issues and events rather than everyday. May you be able to show your insights day by day ... and don't forget that I never slumber or sleep, so even when everyone else was asleep in Gethsemane, I was there, and will be until the dawn."

6. Praying

In the first year of Darius son of Xerxes (a Mede by descent), who was made ruler over the Babylonian kingdom – in the first year of his reign, I, Daniel, understood from the Scriptures, according to the word of the LORD given to Jeremiah the prophet, that the desolation of Jerusalem would last seventy years. So I turned to the LORD God and pleaded with him in prayer and petition, in fasting, and in sackcloth and ashes.
DANIEL 9:1-3

"This, then, is how you should pray:

'Our Father in heaven.
hallowed be your name,
your kingdom come,
your will be done
on earth as it is in heaven.
Give us today our daily bread.
Forgive us our debts,
as we also have forgiven our debtors.
And lead us not into temptation,
but deliver us from the evil one.'

"For if you forgive men when they sin against you, your heavenly father will also forgive you. But if you do not forgive men their sins, your Father will not forgive your sins."

MATTHEW 6:9-15

Devote yourselves to prayer, being watchful and thankful. And pray for us, too, that God may open a door for our message, so that we may proclaim the mystery of Christ, for which I am in chains. Pray that I may proclaim it clearly, as I should. Be wise in the way you act towards outsiders; make the most of every opportunity. Let your conversation be always full of grace, seasoned with salt, so that you may know how to answer everyone.

COLOSSIANS 4:2-6

THROUGHOUT THESE MEDITATIONS the nature and place of prayer has been mentioned. Each meditation has led into prayer and the book itself is intended as an extended dialogue, whether conscious or unconscious. So prayer is not a discrete activity separated from life and worship, but an ever-present aspect of a Christian's daily experience. The central section of the series, "being", leads into the prayer or state of contemplation, and this is intentionally at the heart of things. But prayer is not to be divorced by doing. The placing of a meditation on prayer within the final theme risks giving it connotations that are too specific, not least to do with petitions and supplications. So as we begin let's accept that this is one very little dip into a vast sea already experienced in different ways.

Some of the great moments or experiences are, of course, prayers or answers to prayer. They are the stuff of the exceptional, not the meantime. So what is the nature of prayer day by day as we look ahead to the Day of the Lord? Its essence is that tension between the "now" and the "not yet" of the meantime. The Lord's Prayer puts it perfectly: "Yours is the kingdom" alongside "Your kingdom come". Every prayer is an expression of this paradoxical truth.

The prayer of Daniel comes in one of the most painful meantimes of Jewish history – the seventy years of exile in Babylon. It is the prayer of a man who sees daily prayer as so vital that he has risked life itself to pray with discipline and integrity (Daniel 6:1-10). The prayer is a wrestling with human sin and disobedience, the tragedy of personal and corporate events on the one hand, and God's holiness and grace on the other. There will be times when our prayers tend towards one end of the spectrum more than the other. The Psalms contain every type of prayer and emotion. And they are the best resource for praying in the meantime.

Not long ago a longstanding friend of mine came to see me for counselling or spiritual direction. Part of the discipline we used was to start each session with a psalm or psalms that he had found closest to his own experience or emotions in the preceding week. Never before had I understood just how comprehensive the range is. It is not without reason that communities of faith place the Psalms so centrally in their liturgy and worship.

What transforms the meantime prayer is the assurance that Christ has died and risen, and that he will come again. We pray within that reality and perspective. What we seek is a channelling of the grace and power of God into our daily lives, and at the same time a casting of our cares on him. At times we may wish that the dawn would come before the prayer finishes; at other times the kingdom dawn may be something we have glimpsed and experienced. But over time there will be a balance of the two. This balance will only be achieved with discipline that requires not just regular prayer (as distinct from prayer motivated by problems and crises) but a framework for prayer that emphasises both sides of the paradox.

As I grow older in the faith I become increasingly aware of the frailty of my own prayers, and so come to value the help and traditions of others. The Lord's Prayer is both to be prayed and also a pattern for prayer. When it becomes central to our lives the remarkable effect of such a discipline on the rest of life begins to be seen. It transforms not because of direct answers to prayer or movements of God's Spirit alone, but by bringing order and priorities into our daily lives. It is relevant whether we are under the pressure of busyness, or the worry of emptiness and worthlessness.

Prayer, properly understood, is at the heart of life. It was the hope of Michael Quoist in his *Prayers of Life* that we should so learn to live and to pray that "all life would become a prayer". Thus no action or thought is without its sacramental dimension. There is a place for stillness and contemplation as in Gethsemane. There is also the time: "Get up and let us go!". As we look ahead contemplation leads into purposeful action and the whole, taken together, is best described as prayer. If we have problems with the practice of prayer thus described we can turn afresh to the life of Jesus as portrayed in the Gospels. Prayer is a daily discipline, as with Daniel, but it is also a way of understanding his whole life where every action is a sign of the kingdom and every interaction is also an intersection with the divine presence. "Yours is the Kingdom" – "This also is Thou"; "Your kingdom come" – "Neither is this Thou".

PRAYERS

"Lord,
Whenever I think of prayer, the poverty of my own prayer life becomes immediately apparent. And I suspect (may I confess this?) that others generally don't get very far either. Is it only those in orders and subject to careful discipline who crack it?"

"Child,
The simple answer to your question is 'No'. And as with everything else, some who seem very near the kingdom are actually far away. Whether you can bear another reflection I'm not sure, but the truth is that many who call themselves pagans or unbelievers seem instinctively to understand the nature of prayer; so do children; and women down the ages have integrated feeling, intuition and action more readily than men. But why are you thinking of others when you and I were getting on so well?"

7. Preparing

So David gave orders to assemble the aliens living in Israel, and from among them he appointed stonecutters to prepare dressed stone for building the house of God. He provided a large amount of iron to make nails for the doors of the gateways and for the fittings, and more bronze than could be weighed. He also provided more cedar logs than could be counted, for the Sidonians and Tyrians had brought large numbers of them to David.

David said, "My son Solomon is young and inexperienced, and the house to be built for the LORD should be of great magnificence and fame and splendour in the sight of all the nations. Therefore I will make preparations for it." So David made extensive preparations before his death.

I CHRONICLES 22:2-5

A voice of one calling:
"In the desert prepare
the way for the LORD,
make straight in the wilderness
a highway for our God.
Every valley shall be raised up,
every mountain and hill made low;
the rough ground shall become level,

the rugged places a plain.
And the glory of the LORD will be revealed,
    and all mankind together will see it.
        For the mouth of the LORD has spoken."
ISAIAH 40:3-5

His father Zechariah was filled with the Holy Spirit and prophesied: ...

"And you, my child, will be called a prophet of the Most High;
    for you will go on before the Lord to prepare the way for him,
to give his people the knowledge of salvation
    through the forgiveness of their sins,
because of the tender mercy of our God,
    by which the rising sun will come to us from heaven
to shine on those living in darkness
    and in the shadow of death,
to guide our feet into the path of peace."
LUKE 1:67,76-79

O F ALL THE BIBLICAL characters and heroes, King David ranks as one of the great achievers. He united the nation, defeated many enemies and wrote some of the greatest spiritual songs of all time. Yet, like Moses, there was one great unfulfilled longing. In his case it was the desire to build a temple. (In Moses' case it was lead the people into the Promised Land.) When David realised that the temple was to be built by his great son Solomon he devoted his energy to preparing for the massive project. He procured stone, iron, bronze, wood, gold and silver and also skilled craftsmen. The credit for the temple is always given to Solomon, but the preparations of David should not be overlooked, for without them the great temple would surely have been incomplete in Solomon's reign. As it is the temple was, by common consent, the greatest in Israel's history.

John the Baptist was another of the preparers of history, laying the way for the Messiah himself. When the moment comes and Jesus has been baptised John is imprisoned. Despite his worries and concerns he knows that his task has been done: "He must increase, I must decrease". He is the "Elijah" of whom Malachi wrote in his final words. In fact John represents the whole Old Testament prophetic tradition whose role was to prepare the way for the coming age of the anointed one of God. When Jesus had come, died and been raised from the dead, everything began to fall into place. The whole of Israel's history, worship, tradition and scriptures was a preparation for this person. He gathered up everything in his mission and teaching. He was the lamb of God foreshadowed by every act of Israel's worship; the Great High Priest; the Shepherd; the LORD of Lords and KING of Kings.

Much of our daily life is about preparation. Farmers talk of preparing the ground, but we are familiar with the need to prepare food for cooking, rooms and houses for decoration, orchestras for performances, sports people for competitions, students for exams. Often we underestimate the preparation that goes into the work of others. We assume this is natural talent or ability when there has been painstaking hard work, sometimes years in advance. What goes on behind the scenes is what really counts.

And so it is with the meantime. It is about preparation of everyday things (clothes, food, materials, papers, forms ...) and at the same time can be seen in total as a period of preparation for the future. There is joy, fulfilment, validity in what is done, but there is too the acceptance that everything is pointing beyond the present and what has been already done. Parenthood and teaching are archetypes of this, for what is achieved is always about preparing a child for future roles and situations.

We so overvalue events and achievements we can denigrate the value of preparation and the joy to be found in the process of preparation. How often is the experience of building, learning, shaping, rehearsing together as rewarding (and certainly more fun) than what we think of as the "real" thing. And this is the nub of the issue: we are preparing for a time of unsurpassed and unimaginable joy. Isaiah catches the sense of expectancy and awe in chapter 40:1-5. Yet that doesn't undermine the mundane experience of our daily lives by the contrast: rather, it gathers up that experience because it shows it in a new light. We are building that new city, that new temple, day by day.

PRAYERS

"Lord,
That's timely in any number of ways. It's so easy to become frustrated and to rush the preparation. What dawns on me is that everything on earth is about preparation so 'achievements' and 'completions' are qualitatively no different from preparations in your sight. And when nothing seems to be going on that is at all positive I realise this may be a deeper preparation in your hands."

"Child,
Have you ever thought of the preparation that went into the creation of the world, the universe, the kingfisher's wings, the lichen's chemistry and all of which the parts speak? When people ask me 'how long' in human time scale, I wonder whether they've ever looked at things at all. But there was joy in the preparation even though there will be more joy when all is prepared and the great banquet begins. Another way of seeing it is, 'If this is the scale of the preparations what of the banquet?!'"

8. Hoping

I remember my affliction and my wandering,
the bitterness and the gall.
I well remember them,
and my soul is downcast within me.
Yet this I call to mind
and therefore I have hope;

Because of the LORD's great love we are not consumed,
for his compassions never fail.
They are new every morning;
great is your faithfulness.
I say to myself, "The LORD is my portion;
therefore I will wait for him"
LAMENTATIONS 3:19-24

Therefore, since we have been justified through faith, we have peace with
God through our Lord Jesus Christ, through whom we have gained access
by faith into this grace in which we now stand. And we rejoice in the hope
of the glory of God. Not only so, but we also rejoice in our sufferings,
because we know that suffering produces perseverance; perseverance,
character; and character, hope. And hope does not disappoint us, because

God has poured out his love into our hearts by the Holy Spirit, whom he has given us.

ROMANS 5:1-5

Men swear by someone greater than themselves, and the oath confirms what is said and puts an end to all argument. Because God wanted to make the unchanging nature of his purpose very clear to the heirs of what was promised, he confirmed it with an oath. God did this so that, by two unchangeable things in which it is impossible for God to lie, we who have fled to take hold of the hope offered to us may be greatly encouraged. We have this hope as an anchor for the soul, firm and secure. It enters the inner sanctuary behind the curtain, where Jesus, who went before us, has entered on our behalf. He has become a high priest for ever, in the order of Melchizedek.

HEBREWS 6:16-20

THE POEMS THAT make up the collection of Lamentations come from the period of Jewish history that is perhaps most typical of the meantime – the exile into Babylon. Jerusalem has been destroyed and the future restoration and return seems so far away from reality as to be almost impossible to conceive. The poems are written with a directness and immediacy that conveys a sense of loss, bewilderment, anger and pain. The writer or writers are in limbo grasping for fixed points and it feels like drowning people clutching at straws.

Paul too is writing at a time of suffering and persecution. Both from personal experience and that of his Christian colleagues he knows that suffering produces qualities of character not generated in any other way. In Moscow I had the privilege to be in the presence of Christians who had been imprisoned on account of their faith. Some I watched for hours at close quarters, scrutinising faces, eyes, hands. They had all suffered horribly and yet shining through was a sense of hope and peace. This "meantime" had been the years of communist rule and the gulags. Yet this had produced qualities rare outside such communities.

The hope of Lamentations stems from a fresh understanding of God's nation, his heart revealed through his covenant promises. The hope of Romans and the New Testament looks both backwards and forwards. The meantime is surrounded by the source of hope. We look back to the death and resurrection of Christ. Together these events are the ground of the Christian's hope. By them we are put right with God and assured that God's mightiest act – the raising of Jesus from the dead – is the first-fruit of a harvest beggaring description. We look forward to the time when he will rule everything and everyone in heaven and on earth. The hope we have looks forward confidently to the realisation of all of the covenant promises in a new heaven and earth.

So how does this hope relate to the meantime? It is the author of Hebrews who finds the image that draws things together: hope is the anchor of the soul. The meantime is like a voyage on an ocean where we are far from either the harbour we have left or the one we seek. The weather is unpredictable. It is hard to assess progress. But amazingly in the midst of it all we have an anchor that means we are safe.

That anchor of hope is sorely strained and tested but nothing can dislodge or shift it. The hope is that the meantime has a meaning some of which is known in time, but most of which will become apparent only when time is no more. It draws from the past saving acts of Christ: it means that in the present we can act and live with quiet confidence; it means that at times of greatest storms we can be still, for nothing can separate us from the love of God; it means that we may go astray but never be lost and beyond the reach of our Saviour; and it focuses our minds and hearts on the best which is yet to be.

Some have seen the hope of the Old Testament looking back at God's saving acts and the hope of the New Testament looking forward to the new creation. There is an element of truth in both assertions, but the effect of both in the meantime is that we press ahead with eyes firmly fixed on Jesus the author and finisher of our faith.

"Lord,

Right now the meantime seems manageable. I seize by faith the anchor of hope. But when the storms grow into angry frenzies or when I hit the doldrums and am marooned week in and week out I long for the end, for your saving act to end all acts. Please come quickly."

"Child,

I have come and I am coming. I will not delay one moment longer than is necessary for the preparation to be complete. But in the meantime your hope is secure. You can and will ride out the storms and endure the calms. 'It is good to wait quietly for my salvation.' You have placed your hope in me. You will never be confounded."

Coda

A S IS NOW APPARENT, this book has been gestating for several years and over that time has undergone many revisions at every level. I am grateful for the editors who persuaded me to reshape the whole framework; for friends who have challenged and refined my thinking, and therefore the text, from individual words to complete meditations.

But most of all I am grateful to those many groups and fellowships of every denomination in different parts of the world who have underlined the essential relevance of this book. Whatever anyone has wished their situation might have been, however much people teach otherwise, the fact is that the ordinary Christian life is mostly lived "in the meantime".

I think particularly of that church in East London that I mentioned in the Introduction, and where everyone admitted to living as Christians "in the meantime": unclear about how different aspects of their lives and calling fitted together, trusting God to bring things together, but persevering meanwhile.

Somehow a collective fantasy has prevailed in the church with most of us convinced that in other places or periods, if not in our own, there was tangible blessing, growth and shape to what was happening: that people saw God's will being worked out in their work, family, relationships and church.

At a mealtime in Huntingdonshire some time ago our hostess asked around the table who wanted to read a book like *In the Meantime* because they identified with being in a period of gestation and "in-between-ness". Everyone opted in.

So it will be no great surprise to me after all this reflection and comment to find that many of the readers of this collection will discover a meditation or two that meets them in some respects where they are. Whether it helps is another matter. I have been acutely aware of the inadequacies and particularity of much that I have written. Every time I look at the text I tend to revise it extensively again knowing that it should be better. But at some point it had to be printed and published. My hope is that others will improve upon it and respond faithfully with Scripture to the real life situations of people. But in the meantime here is a personal offering.

And if nothing else in the meditations is of value, then perhaps the reflection that the whole of church history as well as every Christian's life is lived between the two great comings of Jesus: the Incarnation and the Second Coming: will encourage us to realise that even when plans are clear, careers established and when there is a sense of God's infinite presence and direction it is still in the meantime; everything is provisional; we see through a glass darkly, until he come. That will be the end of the meantime, and we will be granted the privilege of seeing how everything fitted together and how, when from a human point of view little or nothing seemed to be happening, from God's perspective the Kingdom of Heaven was steadily advancing in its own way and in his time. Perhaps it is not just that God has his way in the meantime as well as the big events, but that his way of doing things is to operate unobtrusively, when we least expect it or are least aware of his activity.

Acknowledgements

THIS BOOK HAS BEEN so long in the making that its origins lie in the mists of time. I can no longer recall many of those with whom I discussed it and to whom I sent early manuscripts. However, some that I can recall are listed below.

Christine Smith suggested radically reshaping a book on time and life-stages into a series of meditations. There is no way that I would have made this discovery myself and I am so grateful to her.

Carol Cole, who used to help us in the office at Mill Grove and who therefore wrestled daily to decipher my handwriting, was always encouraging about this project. And she insisted that it was among the best things that I had written. As I struggled to focus and refocus my efforts, her enthusiasm triumphed over my doubt.

Mark Philps was the companion with whom I travelled twice to the Soviet Union, and it was with him that the main theme of the book was first discussed. He also kindly proof-read it for me.

Donald Rutherford was as generous in comments on this manuscript as he has been on others that I have sent him. He has been in mind in every paragraph at some stage, although he will realise that I have not always felt able to heed his bidding.

Jan Goodenough was another who read an early script and gave full and insightful comments.

Tony Walter talked with me long and hard about the idea of the book before it underwent the metamorphosis that led to it becoming a collection of meditations. Whether he recognizes the earliest objectives in what has resulted it will be interesting to know!

My family, who were willing to live with me scribbling notes that were to become incorporated into the book at the most unlikely times. One section, for example, was scribbled during half-time at a Saracens rugby match at the Recreation Ground, Bramley Road. It may even have been against Bath, but of that I am unsure! Holidays in Cornwall were not immune either.

The community of Mill Grove has come to put up with me using every spare moment to put more thoughts onto paper.

Spurgeons College invited me to lecture there in 1978 and I continued for thirty years, during which time many of the themes here germinated.

Students around the world have helped me to see the variety of cultural perspectives on the themes.

Many, many literary sources, most I hope acknowledged, but some no doubt unconscious.

I thank Tony Cantale and Andy Bisgrove for seeing what it might become, and Tony for his photos and design.

Church fellowships, families and individuals around the world who have shared their stories, hopes, dreams and fears with me so openly that I knew the book had to see the light of day despite its obvious imperfections.

Those who have asked me for copies of the manuscript as they were struggling with the meantime, sometimes against what seemed like insuperable odds.

Doris Kearns and Adrian Turl, who proof-read the text and mused over it with me.

Ruth, who as ever bore it all so patiently, including a holiday in North Wales when I finally decided to go for it, rather than make a trip with her to Bardsey.

Lightning Source UK Ltd.
Milton Keynes UK
UKOW041641101212

203451UK00001B/75/P